Publicists Tips & Tricks

How To Promote and Market Your Book

MADI PREDA

AuthorsPR

How to Promote
And
Market Your Book

Copyright ©Madi Preda 2014

How to Promote and Market Your Book

Publicists Secrets, Tips, and Tricks

ISBN 13 - 978-1500228644

ISBN 10 -   1500228648

Cover Art – Authors PR Madi Preda

Edited by Nancy King PhD

To YOU, yes I am talking with you, the one who is reading this book right now. I hope you will find the information useful and I would love to hear from you.

To my husband Patrick, for his support and to the two authors who trusted me in the very beginning: Sharon Kay Roberts and Roy Dimond and to all the wonderful people from the social media platforms and Wordpress bloggers.

Thank you all,

Madi

"A book is not only a friend, it makes friends for you. When you have possessed a book with mind and spirit, you are enriched. But when you pass it on you are enriched threefold."

-Henry Miller

Letter from the author

How I started my journey in the book business

There was a time in my life when everything around me began to fall apart. It was a time when I realized that I had too much time in my hands and nothing else to do besides the usual housecleaning, cooking, etc. My brain started shouting at me that it needed some other activities in order to keep its capacities and neurons intact. I can't say I was listening to my inner voice; it was more an emergency call.

I was lucky enough to find some people who trusted me and gave me the chance to do something that I really like; reading and marketing books. Along the way, I had the opportunity to meet wonderful writers and wonderful characters.

I thought this was a good time for an investment of time and no money at all. Not only that, but the joy of discovering good books and interviewing writers, being able to think about the message of the book based on talks with the author, made me want to do more and more on a daily basis.

I decided to pursue this advertising and marketing business by doing PR for writers who might well become part of my online community.

I hope that some of you will visit me at

Authors PR Madi Preda – http://authorspr.tripod.com/ or

AUTHORS PROMOTION - http://authorspromotion.wordpress.com and the fan page for this book https://www.facebook.com/bookspromotion

I am happy to hear from you whether you visit my website to book my services or for a chat and some freebies (yes, I still have such things there). I am always happy to hear from you.

What is spinning in my mind these days after writing this book is both the issue of selling it, and how or if it will resonate with readers. I knew my target audience from the beginning so thinking now about my book being in the hand of writers with years of experience gives me goose bumps. In my case it was an experiment to see if I am walking on the right path with my advertising campaigns. While writing I tried to put myself in other writers' shoes, and consider uncertainties, anxieties, and doubts that writers have. I know that is not easy to be a writer. I began doing publicity as a way of helping writers to find their market at a time when I was feeling unsure about myself and I never dreamed about writing a book.

There is something driving my writing that has to be expressed for the project to be realized. To me, the value of this book is determined by whether the strategies I suggest are effective or not because this is the meaning of *How To Promote and Market Your Book.*

Madi Preda – Authors PR authorspr@gmail.com

TABLE OF CONTENT

PART ONE

PART TWO

-Where to send press releases

-Editors

-General Fiction Bloggers

-Adventure, Mystery, Thriller Bloggers

-Sites to Promote free and discounted books

-Facebook Groups and Pages

-News Portals and Archives

INTRODUCTION

"A book's marketing implies strategy and creativity."

~Madi Preda

Have you ever wondered why some authors make a fortune on their writing while so many others who have written wonderful books seem to struggle?

The answer is quite simple. You can do your own marketing as well, without a lot of expense, but with a bit of hard work. Marketing and promoting are not so difficult if you have enthusiasm and determination, and you know what to do and how to do it.

This handbook will help you to make the right choices and will show you how to start to promote your book yourself. It is useful for people who have just started a business of marketing books, as well as for writers who choose to do it for their own books.

How to Promote and Market Your Book is based on my experience as a publicist. It is written in an easy to understand and friendly way, explaining step by step what to do in order to get your book to readers, marketing trends, and how to make them work to develop your brand as an author and improve sales.

Part one of the book offers general suggestions, how-to advice, templates, lists of agents, reviewers, bloggers, and sites for promotion, periodicals or literary journals and radio shows, information on fundamentals of publicity, and effective online marketing campaigns (case study for a children's book).

The topics include setting goals, approaching media, writing newsworthy marketing content, and samples of press releases or blurbs for different types of campaigns.

I have written this book for writers who may have only a little experience in marketing and public relations, but a huge amount determination to succeed, just like you and me.

Part two of the book presents a theoretical case study of a marketing campaign for xxxxxxxxxxxxxx xxxxxxxxxxxxxxx, by Xxxxxxx Xxxxxxxx, a book on bullying, discrimination, and community responsibilities, and a case study on a publicity campaign for *Changing Spaces* by Nancy King, a novel that explores the possibility of re-inventing one's self after a long marriage and an unexpected divorce.

The major purpose of marketing is to determine which type of content is most likely to have an impact on consumers' behavior and decisions. Marketing research proves that consumers react to credible content and independent user reviews when making buying decisions.

Identifying the most effective types of content to inform consumers is one of the difficult tasks of marketing for any kind of product and even more when it comes to marketing books. One thing to keep in mind is that *trust matters* and it is crucial to gain the audience's trust.

A short analysis of different types of content will make it easier to understand the impact of each type on the consumer's purchase decision.

- Expert content: articles and reviews from an expert in writing or the genre of the book

- Branded content: content produced by the author

- Users' content: such as reviewers from Amazon, Goodreads, or bloggers.

The audience's decision to purchase a specific book is based on familiarity with the author's books, settings of the action, or the subject of the book, and on the affinity for the author or the book genre. Different types of marketing content will generate different types of reactions. If you produce good content, and a wide variety of it, there are more chances to succeed.

Expert marketing Content: Articles from journalists or even the author's articles published in reputable newspapers or magazines will have more credibility than an article on an author's blog.

Branded content: Not everyone has the chance to be interviewed by a reputable journalist. What does one do in this case? Marketing content produced by the author is better received by a reader if it is posted by a third party source such as an interview, or a guest post on someone else's blog. Research shows that this will influence the reader's decision to purchase a book more than the same content published on an author's website or blog.

Users' content: Reviews or a little promotional spot by a blogger will influence readers' purchasing decisions. The more placements for your book the better will be the results.

The conclusion for this short analysis is that in order to build trust and influence readers' behaviour to buy a book, it is better to start with credible expert content, move on with branded content to connect with social media, and then to engage and use media network for user content.

Maintain your efforts by encouraging your social media network to share your story and your marketing content. Try different approaches and different types of content until you find out what works best for your book.

Seeking advance book reviews: Build the foundation for launching your book. The manuscript of your book is edited and ready to publish. With today's technology, you could have the book on sale in a matter of days. But if you want to secure advance reviews and prepare the release of your dream you have to wait and start looking for advance reviews. Reading takes time and so does getting a review.

Third-party endorsements for a book help to build credibility for your book and springboard the launch. Having a number of reviews makes a difference in book sales, increases the book's rank, and adds credibility. Reviews matter to readers and media when they check out a book. Reviews also matter to Amazon ratings and play a role with many book promotion sites. Some of them offer free promotion if you have a certain number of reviews.

For an indie writer, sending out ARCs—Advance Review Copies—is important. Nobody has a standard number or a magic way to get reviews so aim to get as many reviews as you possibly can. Time will tell you that your efforts were worth it.

Target reviewers in your genre: Look for people who specialize in, or have an affinity for your genre. It takes a lot of time to find the right bloggers and submit your ARC according to their review policy. Post information about your book on your social media network and see if your contacts are willing to do a review for you.

ARC giveaways on Goodreads and LibraryThing are a good idea. Don't expect that everyone who won a copy will post a review; the statistics says that only 20 – 25 % post reviews but even so this is quite a good return. Find the right contacts, send the right content, and then, be prepared to wait for a while.

While waiting, the best thing to do is to plan your online marketing campaign.

Planning your digital marketing campaign

If you plan a journey to a new destination, you either need a map or you download driving directions.

Let's think in similar terms about marketing a book. You need to plan a successful strategy to get the book to readers. The map for any book promotion, for any product in fact, is a marketing plan, which includes your goals, how, and what to say to whom, and where to find the right audience.

Goals provide a target, something to which you aspire, a means for a particular activity. We need to ask why we do what we do. Is it because we want to progress, to improve a standard, to look back and say, "Yes, I've done something in my life". We all have to find our own motivation.

When you set your goals, be realistic. Make sure you can reach them over a certain period of time. Think twice about what is possible to achieve and then build the marketing plan around it. In a poetic way, meeting your goals will transform your dreams into reality.

The strategy you develop creates a way to sell your book to a particular category of readers in concordance with their preferences.

How you can transform yourself from an author into a successful writer? Embark with me on this journey and I hope that my experience will help you find your way to market your book successfully.

"You can write the most wonderful book in the world. But if people don't know about your book they won't know to buy it."

~Madi Preda

What is marketing?

When you began your writing journey you started by feeling that you had a story to tell that you wanted to share with the world. You probably didn't think how difficult it would be to let people know about your book.

Marketing is related to consumer's needs. These days publishers expect you to market your book yourself. You, the author, are responsible for publicizing your book to make it successful. Although it is difficult to be noticed in today's tough, competitive market place, now that your book has been published, your job is to develop the tools to make your book a success, to attract an audience, to make readers want to buy it.

What might make a reader want to buy your book? What's in it for them? Who is your audience? How do you catch the attention of your audience and keep it? Why should they buy your book?

You need to be sure that you bring something new to your readers, something that triggers their emotional and psychological interest, which can satisfy their needs.

Social media marketing is designed to promote. When you advertise a book and create a social and personal connection, you make readers notice you and want to buy your book. If your connection with readers is strong enough, they may read other books by you or look for the next one. If you manage to do this, you are a WINNER.

You simply need to be sociable and friendly.

The success does not happen accidentally

It is not just about writing a good book and your publisher sending press releases. It is about developing relationships with readers and building an author brand. We all know that a successful book is not just about writing but creating exposure in the

marketplace as well as an effective online presence. Give your book the chance that it deserves. This is the way to success.

You wrote a book and now the pages between the book covers need to be highlighted throughout your publicity campaign and communicated in a unique way that resonates with readers and media.

It is like a tale of a dancer who has the music but needs someone to play it in order to perform. You can make the dance go viral with the help of interested readers.

Your strategy defines your target-market decisions. Targets respond to promotional strategies in different ways. You can't approach media in the same way you approach readers. You need to learn how to present your book specifically for each one of your targets.

Continuous improvement is necessary. Following the strategic directions will reward your efforts and help you to become effective and efficient, not only as a writer but as a marketer as well. Take time to think about what you can do to implement your strategies, and achieve your goals.

There are four major steps of a book production: publishing, distribution, marketing, and promotion, and on top of these a self-published author has to take into consideration the cost of editing, cover designs and formatting. Even if the publisher is covering these costs, the author needs to be involved as much as possible to insure the finished book reflects the author's intent.

A few major steps you should follow when you send out your book proposal to an agent or publisher

What is the book about?

Give a clear idea about the book in the very beginning if you want your proposal to be read. You need to present what is most catching about your book in a couple of sentences.

Whom do you address?

Who is your target audience, what will you give them that is interesting and new. You can compare your book with others in the same genre and mention what are the new approaches of the subject, a few conclusions and how the story will influence the target readers.

Create yourself a good biography

A biography should be included in your submission but do yourself a favor and don't start telling them about cats and dogs and how much you love your family or how many children do you have.

Agents, publishers and media outlets want to hear about you as a writer, have you been published, where and when, do you won any awards, do you have a strong relationship with some radio or TV Shows, are you a contributor to some literary publications, magazines or newspapers?

What experience gave you credit to write about this particular subject and anything else you can think of which will recommend you as the right author for such a book, subject and genre.

What is your marketing plan?

This should be realistic and specific; you may know specialized publications that might be interested to put on an article or some radio shows that you have been in contact with in the past.

How do you see cross promotion in accordance with your subject and what are you going to do in terms of pre-pub promotion, before your book is out on the market (blog tour for cover reveal, free chapters uploaded on specialized sites, building or developing your author platform, website, blog, social media accounts).

Express your intention of setting – up a **pre-order campaign** and giveaway, mention a few major reviewers where do you intend to send galleys or ARC, and specify what your intentions are about.

Publicity after the release date

You still have to work just as hard when the book is out on the market, and this is exactly what you should do and what a publisher wants to hear. Tell them about asking for reviews, fan pages created, speaking engagement in your local libraries, launch parties if you are going to do such a thing.

You can organize a virtual tour in advance for the release day and tell them how many sign – ups do you have or if you have the intention to find a publicist to do all of this for you. If so say a few words about the publicist, a few authors who were promoted by him/her, mention a book which is successful because this publicist efforts.

Advantages of being represented by an agent

Literary agents connect authors and publishers, and negotiate the contract for you A good and experienced agent knows the market, and can offer advice and guidance, advising an author on various aspects. What a literary agent can do for you and how they can help? A literary agent has many contacts in this tough publishing business and even he/she will not represent you, they can help with an advice or a recommendation that means a lot . Don't think about a literary agent as being someone with superpower and don't be afraid to ask for advice or suggestion. I met agents saying I am busy now or I don't represent this genre anymore but I can recommend you to contact …that person.

This was happening to me with a very nice person who was retired by the time I contacted her and she very kindly recommend me someone else. Since then we are in touch and is a pleasure to have a chat with her from time to time, not necessarily about publishing books.

Advantages of working with small publishers

By working with small press, authors will get a lot of attention from the editors and designers. With small press, you can talk about a writer-editor relationship, and a lot more publicity. This doesn't means that you will not benefit of all these services from the main stream press, just let's think about what I said in the beginning of this book, set achievable and realistic goals.

A small press is the step into bigger things and we know that saying – A 1000 miles journey begins with one-step.

Jenene D. Scott

Author/Publisher for A Book's Mind

Tips from a Publisher, with the Heart of a Writer

Congratulations! You wrote a book and are among the select few that have become "published." I hope you took time to celebrate. Most writers lack the fortitude and confidence to make it this far. Chances are you are basking in your new found title of *published author* and are selling books to every family member, neighbor, and friend you can possibly solicit. You have joyfully spread the word of your newfound achievement with anyone that will listen.

What happens when sales abruptly stop? What about the boxes of books in the garage? How do you reach the people outside of your bubble of influence? You may feel as if your dream of becoming a successful author is about to pop. Your day job, and its steady income, are looking increasingly appealing. How do I know? I've been there.

This is a pivotal crossroads moment and there is only one way to make sure you take the right path.

It's time to evaluate your desired outcome.

Is this a hobby? Are you satisfied with your work being read and appreciated only by those closest to you? Without giving writing a second thought, can you take it or leave it?

I am guessing the answer is, *No*. It was for me.

Most authors fall into two categories. They are either passionate about making money or a difference. What is the secret to your success…? Are you ready? Take notes on this…you need to be passionate about both!

Reality check! Publishing a book is equivalent to opening a small business.

Let's say you make the best cupcakes that have ever touched the lips of mankind. You open a small shop because you want to share your talent with the world. Is that enough? But you say, "I'm a baker, not an advertising specialist, I don't like keeping track of finances or working the cash register. That hinders me from doing what I love most. I'm going to spend my days doing what I do best, baking and nothing else. People will come because my cupcakes are simply, the best!"

Does that sound like a successful business plan? Would you become partners with this person? How long will it take for people to taste what they are missing? Unless you or your best friend already have celebrity status, I'm guessing you will run out of money to pay the rent before the good news gets around.

I'm sure your plan is to hire someone to do all the tedious things needed to keep your business going. Wonderful, do it as soon as you can! But meanwhile, in the real world, consider it *your* job.

As writers, we have fantasies of landing a big contract with a publishing house and turning over our book while they do all the work. Think again! That's not how traditional publishing works. You still have to generate sales because if your book sales don't meet their business goals, they can discontinue promotion and distribution of your book.

Are you convinced that marketing is important? I hope so, because if it's not important to you, who is going to sell your books?

This leads to the obvious question, "How do I build my successful book business?"

This is the biggest mistake I see as a Publisher. Authors strive to market their book! Reality check!

Don't market your book, *market you!*

Readers follow authors, not books. When they are finished reading your masterpiece and want more, what will they type in the online search box? The author's name. *Your name.* All of your promoting should be centered on you. After all, without you there is no book!

How do you get your name out there? Good question.

In today's world it is all about Social Media and Social Networking.

Social Media is communication through digital means, such as websites, Facebook, Twitter, Pinterest, blog sites like Wordpress or Blogger, Linkedin, and online stores like Amazon or eBay, photo and video sharing sites or phone apps such as YouTube or Instagram.

Social Networking uses social media as a platform to engage relationships through instant sharing of information. This gives you, the author, a voice and a way to communicate with peers, customers and potential readers. These are all free opportunities that open access to more people and relationships quicker and easier than ever before.

Where should you start? It doesn't matter. Starting is the key. However, if I had to choose, Facebook is by far the world's leader in social media with the most active users than any other site. Once you create a main account, open an author's page under your pen name and invite your friends to join. It's an easy place to begin.

Once you venture into this fast paced digital world, you need to know the secret to success. Are you still taking notes? The word is, *consistency*! When you blog and post, you need to do it on a regular basis. Make it a part of your routine. Use sites such as Hootsuite to combine your media and give you the ability to schedule posts to go live even when you are away from the computer. Have something interesting and relevant to say. Search your heart for things you are most passionate about and share them with your followers. If you find it helpful, chances are someone else will too.

If you found this all very daunting, and the thought of venturing into the digital world makes you break out into a cold sweat, ask for help. Everyone knows someone that always has their nose to a cell phone or behind a laptop. You know, the ones that line up to buy the latest and greatest gadget before you knew it existed. Call that person, ask for help. It is simple for those who know what they are doing, to get you up and going. Even though your business is all about you as an author, it takes a team to sustain your business.

I wish this article was all about wishing hard and watching success drop into your lap. However, I think we all know that is not how life works. We pay our dues, put in hard work, and then reap the rewards. In the end, as cliché as it sounds, you need to fulfill your dreams and you can make that happen.

Now get back to work. You have things to do!

To show you I practice what I preach, for more tips on writing and publishing, and to schedule a Writers Information Seminar, you can find me at the following…

Facebook: https://www.facebook.com/jdscottnovels?ref=hl

Blog: http://jdscottnovels.wordpress.com/

Twitter: https://twitter.com/JDScott_Author

Website: www.jdscottnovels.com

Publishing: www.abooksmind.com

Email: Jenene@abooksmind.com

J.D. Scott BIO

J.D. Scott is the organizing member of Abba's Writers and The Skulls: Publish Focused Group

in Phoenix, Arizona. She leads, organizes, and teaches both critiquing and story content/ development to its members

In 2013, J.D. Scott became part of the team at *A Book's Mind* as a Publisher. She enjoys working alongside writers, helping them fulfill their dreams of becoming published authors.

Before being bit by the writing bug, J.D. Scott spent 20 years working with children as a nanny, mentor, camp counselor, and youth group leader. With a heart for today's youth, she set out to write books that both entertain and inspire them to rise above the current culture and see their true value.

If you choose self-publishing, I highly recommend having a look at www.ingramspark.com

Why IngramSpark^{SM} — and what it means for your books

IngramSpark is the only publishing platform that delivers fully integrated print and digital distribution services. A relationship with IngramSpark will let you to focus on your writing process while they manage the other chores: printing, shipping, and distribution.

IngramSpark will connect your book to major e-book retailers, like Amazon Kindle, iBooks, and Kobo and many others emerging e-book retailers. That is giving you more time to do what you do best…write and let them to do what they do best.

While I was doing publicity for someone, the person asked if I was successful, if she had sold more books after the campaign. Her question is translated in Marketing as ROI analyze.

Marketing ROI

ROI means **Return On Investment**. It is not so easy to measure this since you not only invest some money, you also invest a lot of time, which is difficult to quantify.

With every action that we take, we wait for something in return. Moreover, this is exactly what you do when marketing your book. Authors need to understand that marketing and advertising, especially online, takes time. This doesn't necessarily generate profit right away, but it generates prestige and recognition for your author's brand and for your book.

I know that everyone expects high returns, but if you have your books in a bookshop you don't expect that the next day the seller will call you to say he sold all the books. Why should you expect that from a publicist or from yourself if you are the one who is promoting your books? You need to define marketing and promotion as an investment in time and dedication, with the hope that later on you will see a return on your investment.

If all a writer can think of is sales, the answer is simple. Convince a distributor to take on your books and then that company will be responsible for the sales of your book.

A publicist or marketer is working for your book and your brand every day. Creating promotional materials, contacting media, readers, booksellers, bloggers, etc. takes time, energy, and money. I am sure that you will agree with me if you do your own promotion.

Publicists have finished their job when they have kept their promises and done what they said they would do. You can judge the results by checking the search engines, and if you are looking for your name or for your book, there should be a few pages about your brand and your title. If the publicist managed to engage you for a few interviews, had a few mentions in newspapers or magazines, a successful blog tour, or found a few booksellers who were interested in your book, that means there was a successful campaign.

In my experience, I booked two writers, whom I appreciate very much, with a prestigious radio station. I couldn't find a more righteous pitch for that book. However, to finalize it took me six months. Fortunately, since we were still working together we could do it and everyone was pleased with the results. That is why I say don't confuse marketing with sales. Marketing for me is more about placements than about sales.

Unfortunately, marketing is often the first budget that is cut when times are tough, but at least try to do it for yourself by spending within your budget.

"You don't stop the watch when you are afraid of getting old, so don't cut off advertising when you want to save money."

~Madi Preda

I promise you that I will follow my own advice if you will do the same.

Public Relations for Writers

Public Relations means getting authors mentioned on radio, doing book tours, or of placing an author's books media in any form—print, radio, online, or television.

As a publicist in this changing world of digital marketing, I understood that more than anything, PR means communicating your message at the right time, to the right audience, in the right place.

As a PR agent for writers, or if you are doing it yourself, public relations focuses on building good relationship with different audience, obtaining favorable publicity, and building a good public image for the author. In essence, the PR agent needs to talk with the right audience in the right tone of voice to build the author's brand perception.

Public relation is an integral part of marketing strategy, which carries out to a message to diverse categories of the public: readers, distributors, journalists, and social media networks. These messages can be communicated across the world, online or offline, but they must be crafted smartly and interestingly to make a difference, generate traffic, and drive sales. They are key messages that follow the marketing plan for promoting and build the author's reputation.

Doing public relations, you shape audience's perception about the author. In my interviews, I always prefer to talk with authors, more about themselves, than the book, and do a promotional spot concentrated on the story afterwards. This way I help the readers to know a little about the author, their personalities, perceptions, and thoughts on life's issues. I think revealing the author's thoughts makes readers feel closer to the writer because they see that the author isn't just someone who wants to sell them stories, but is someone who has learned from experience, someone like them who has a story to share.

When you do public relations keep in mind a few factors:

- You share information and stories that are worthy of sharing, which have an impact on your audience.

- You tell the story through emotions and human experience with which readers can connect.

- Your duty is to protect the reputation of an author and his/her book, and build and maintain a good public image for the brand and the work.

Be sure you get and offer attention:

When you pitch media, make it clear why the material should be of interest to the publication audience, and if possible, read articles about the person with whom you plan to contact. Making a short mention "I've seen your article about . . . and I thought you might be interested in . . . will help you connect with the person. He/she will probably be pleased that you have done your homework, which helps you to be considered as a person who knows what she is talking about.

- Be accessible by using different ways of communication on various devices.

- Provide useful information and support if someone contacts you.

- Try to build long-term relationships. This makes it possible to reach your contacts when you need them and make the connection more reciprocal.

- Make your company or the author's brand stand out from a marketing perspective.

- Respect online etiquette and don't send mass emails.

- Send a thank you note every time you receive a mention and share the article, favorite the tweet, or like the Facebook post.

- Build a good relationship with other writers and bloggers, which works both ways; you offer support and they may do the same for you.

Marketing and PR

"Writing a book without promoting it is like waving to someone in a dark room. You know what have you done but nobody else does."

~Madi Preda

Marketing and PR work best if they are used together. I can't imagine doing one without the other.

While marketing requires doing market research, exploring, creating, and supplying information and products to fit the needs of a target market, public relations has to do with reporting the news and promoting a new product and brand. Marketing creates responses that PR can respond to by attracting consumers' resources, and driving sales.

Both of these deal with the end product (book in our case) at the end of a certain activity (the writing process). The purpose of marketing strategies is to bring to market a book by presenting it in a way that the audience will buy it. Promoting a book is about everything from market research to advertising and PR aims to build a relationship with current and potential customers, and then create the pathway that will expand the market. There is a saying: **"PR lights the fire. Marketing fans the flames" ~ Al Ries**

It is hard to separate the two because they actually stand under the same umbrella. All forms of communication are more or less integrated and involve all available tools to sell what customers are looking to buy. You have what the readers want—the book—and you need to make a plan that motivates them to buy it. Writers want and need exposure in order to gain readers for their books.

Effective publicists think from the reader's point of view and ask themselves: "What's in it for them?" Then the public relations person works to influence their behaviour and motivate an individual or a group to buy the book by creating interest and engagement with the subject matter.

While some professionals make distinctions between marketing and PR, they all see them as related and use them together as the most effective way to build and engage the target audience.

Today I felt like changing my author hat with the publicist one and I thought well, what should I say about my book? How I can find an original way to promote and engage?

Here is what I came up with: a universal post that you can use for pitching media, a book proposal, and promotional spots for a blog post, as a source for synopsis and press release It can also help with the marketing plan as well or can be used as an editorial review.

I will be happy if some of you contact me and tell me your opinion about it. You can reach me at authorspromotion@gmail.com or through the form on my website http://authorspr.tripod.com. I look forward to hearing your response as well as ideas about whether you think it will sell my book.

CASE STUDY – Editorial Review

How to Promote and Market Your Book by Madi Preda

Practical Guide to Transform Your Book in a successful one

About the author: Madi Preda is a freelance publicist who started doing promotion for books and writers when her husband published his two novels. She has created publicity campaigns for many writers, traditional or self-published, publicizing more than 50 books within a year of launching her first campaign. Her mission is to help authors by using a variety of means, and to gain exposure and media coverage through her online marketing campaigns. Because of her experience, she decided to write a practical guide for authors or beginners in marketing, by explaining step-by-step, how to make market a book successfully.

Who is it For: Any author who wants to create and launch a successful book or people who decide to run an online business doing book promotion.

What It Will Help You Do: This guide walks you through the development of an author's brand and suggests ways to improve book sales. Madi covers a wide range of topics: brainstorming, marketing plans for different genres, figuring out your target market and the right niche, designing a website or a media press kit, dealing with social media, using email marketing and having a memorable launch.

What's Included: This efficient guide includes three comprehensive case studies on marketing and PR campaign that are full of smart and efficient ideas, detailed strategies with links, worksheets and checklists. You won't just receive the information — the case studies will analyze the campaign and the target audience, media pitch and book tour.

The Best Part: Reading through her book is like chatting with a friend—one who knows her stuff and tries to present it in a very approachable way.

Her book contains valuable resource lists such as: book bloggers, publishers, literary agents, newspapers and magazines, independent booksellers, Facebook groups, sites to promote books, and radio shows for authors. Following her lists you can pitch media, request an interview, send newsletters to booksellers, and set up your own virtual tour.

She uses personal experience as a publicist to help you connect with her, and she takes the time to walk you through the whole process. Get ready! **This book is definitely not your typical online business book**: It is part business, part personal coaching, part lessons, and a lot of love for the written word.

What Would Make It Even Better: Your coming up with suggestions about what you would like her to talk about in her next book

How It will Help You: You will get to know Madi's personality and gain a friend who is always ready to help you with advice about setting up your campaign. While reading her words she hopes you will ask yourself—"Why wait? Why not start promoting my book? Madi's suggestions, information and advice make it sound possible. I will give it a try."

You might feel that this is impossible, but I say it is possible. Madi lives in Greece and doesn't speak Greek, apart of necessary conversation at the market place. Because of that she made her contacts around the world with English speakers. All her contacts are online. She starts her day in pajamas with a nice cup of coffee and her laptop, yet this is her job. If you don't believe this just Google Authors PR Madi Preda and see what comes up or visit her website http://authorspr.tripod.com/ or her blog http://authorspromotion.wordpress.com

Recommendation: If you are looking for a fun-loving and creative friend to be on your side while you promote your book, this book will be your new best friend. If you'd prefer a grammatically polished business manual, written on an academic level, then you'd be better off buying something else.

*If you pre-order **How to Promote and Market Your Book**, you are supporting **Authors PR** and will win a free 30 minute consultation with Madi, who will answer your questions and concerns about your book promotion.*

Thank You,

Madi Preda Authors PR

How to create a Marketing Plan

Start doing research, making notes, and setting goals.

You have a book and it is a wonderful story. What is next?

Research

Examine other successful books in your genre. What is it that catches your attention and makes you want to read that book? Use this for your marketing plan and campaign.

Who are reviewers for this book? You can contact them saying that you have seen their review for a book in the same genre and ask if they would like to review yours as well. Tell them about the strengths of your book and what it brings that is new and exciting to readers.

Try to find contacts such as independent booksellers. You can do this by joining websites for independent writers, reading other blogs and searching websites that have a writer's resources' page. If you can join a writers association this is a big achievement; some of them specialize and focus on specific genres or locations.

Branding

You want to reach as many readers as you can and in order to do this you'll need to have a strong online presence on as many networks you can reach. Begin with the most popular ones: LinkedIn, GoodReads, Book Blogs, Ning, Authonomy, AuthorsDen as well as many others.

Set up a blog for yourself on WordPress or Blogger, which puts your posts immediately on Google pages. On Google + and Yahoo Groups you can join groups, communities, book clubs, other writers, and readers.

Set up an email address if possible with an integrated marketing system such as Constant Contact, MPZ Mail, or others that give you the possibility of building your email subscribers list and sending newsletters in one bunch.

If you choose WordPress or Blogger to set up a blog, you can link the blog with your Google+, LinkedIn, or Tumblr account and all of your posts will show up there automatically.

Strategy

Sending out ARCs or Galleys is a very good strategy when doing a pre-pub campaign. They are provided free to reputable sources for reviews, such as: literary journals, magazines, newspapers, and professional reviewers. Almost all of them want to be contacted three or four months before the book is released. You can put some of them on the back cover when it is printed.

In addition, you can ask for reviews from book clubs member or bloggers in advance but make sure to tell them the probable release date.

There is a big community of librarians on Authonomy and if you post some free chapters, if you are lucky enough, you might convince them to put your book in their library.

Part of the strategy is knowing how to plan the subsequent steps that will generate sales for your book. For this, you need to count advertising, promotion, and social media.

Case study – Marketing Plan for Children's Books

Summary

Marketing Plan developed for xxxxxxxxxxxx by xxxxxxxxxx

xxxxxxxxxx series – A collection of three books

- xxxxxxxxxx xxxxxxxxxx

-yyyyyyyy yyyyyyyyyyyyyy

- *zzzzzzzzz zzzzzzzzzz*

The collection is meant to delight and engage young children, ages . . . , to have fun while reading or be read to as part of their bedtime story experience. Each story has an educational message and a surprising ending.

What is a SWOT analysis?

SWOT sounds like a foreign language for some people, but is actually a very simple way to identify few attributes of a book or any other product.

S – Strengths

W – Weaknesses

O – Opportunities

T – Threats

These are attributes that you need to analyze by comparing them with other books in the same genre, and relating them to your target market.

SWOT Analysis of . . .

--Colorful illustration and attractive name of the characters.

--Educational message introduced to children through the toys' world.

--Interesting settings like Zoo, Aquarium, The Toys Museum, which will become a place to advertise and sell the books.

--Interesting points about how people take care of the animals and how toys have feelings like people.

--For the scholastic market, the series has a BIC code classification.

Opportunities:

--The collection may attract attention from associations that support children's literacy and could be useful in nurseries, kindergartens, prep schools, or for use by parents who want to encourage their children to widen their reading experience.

--Included are activities and reading tips for teachers and parents, guided reading in classrooms, learning bags, and day-by-day reading boxes.

--The book can be used as a present for tea parties, birthday celebrations, and open days at libraries or schools.

--It is a good idea to start the publicity campaign before the school year starts, when meetings with parents take place, as an opportunity to include the books in the new school year curricula.

--Present the books at meetings at local schools, kindergartens, and other places where a fan club can be created. The collection can be presented together with coloring sheets for the characters of each story.

--Consider having books available at party venues for children and entertainers at children's parties, playgrounds and after school programs.

--Try to place books with independent booksellers who specialize in children books (i.e. Scholastic).

--Starting an aggressive campaign from the beginning will give you or the publisher time to see if sales are increasing so there can be reprints in time for seasonal sales.

--Contact chain stores and find the right staff members to provide credible guidance.

Target market and positioning – All of the above

Promotion:

--Organize in-store displays and promotional materials.

- For children's clubs and party venues, create a fan club, color sheets and award certificates for the best reader of the day, the hungry reader of the week, and the child who has read a certain number of stories from the collection.

- Schedule storytelling sessions with local bookstores, schools, and libraries. If possible, find some students, actors, philologists, or community members who want to volunteer their time for children's entertainment.

- Print posters, flyers and bookmarks to highlight the location, coloring pages and award certificates.

- Print business cards with the book's ISBN number, and contact info and give them to every location related with children activities.

- Contact children's theaters and performances so that you can eventually make a partnering agreement and/or sub rights sale contract.

- Contact animators and actors organizations dedicated to encourage young children by performing.

- Contact online communities for parents and present the collection to them.

- Print a few coloring pages with your characters and offer them everywhere—party venues, toy stores, pediatric doctor's waiting room, even offer them to children in the park. (Sounds silly maybe but it works, believe me)

Children's books bloggers

All Things Jill-Elizabeth
http://www.Jill-Elizabeth.com

Books Kids Like
http://www.bookskidslike.blogspot.com

educationdiva
educationdiva.com

Holly's Check It Out Book List
http://hollyscheckitout.blogspot.com/

Just Children's Books
http://www.justchildrensbooks.com

Kid Book Ratings
http://kidbookratings.blogspot.com

KidsRead
kidsread.wordpress.com

Novels On The Run
www.novelsontherun.blogspot.com

Page-turner
pageturnerby-beth.blogspot.com

Read it Again, Mama!
http://www.readitagainmama.blogspot.com

Story Quest Children's Books
www.storyquestbooks.com

KIDS RELATED WEBSITES – UK

www.netmums.com

www.all4kidsuk.com

www.parentsdirectories.com

www.babydirectory.com

www.planetparty.co.uk

www.thepartybook.co.uk

www.northlondonmums.com

www.familiesonline.co.uk

www.freeindex.co.uk

www.whatson4kidsparties.co.uk

www.mummymondays.co.uk

www.childfriendly.co.uk

www.essexmums.org

www.magicpencil.co.uk

www.treasureislandtoys.co.uk

www.bestkidsparty.co.uk

www.thepartysupplies.co.uk

www.childrenspartyentertainers.org.uk

Google + Communities

https://plus.google.com/u/0/communities/111369404544048701925

https://plus.google.com/u/0/communities/114772293552987924264

https://plus.google.com/u/0/communities/115695483493018727478

https://plus.google.com/u/0/communities/101620624583494034335

https://plus.google.com/u/0/communities/118300969551868529539

https://plus.google.com/u/0/communities/113041725517167869706

https://plus.google.com/u/0/b/115612912489755160221/
communities/101304402264310213372

https://plus.google.com/u/0/b/115612912489755160221/
communities/110985536536226557204

Children's Magazines

Parents Magazine http://www.parents.com/

Underneath The Juniper Tree https://plus.google.com/u/0/113111789856642510763

Facebook Groups for Children's Books

https://www.facebook.com/profile.php?id=419730644746044

https://www.facebook.com/profile.php?id=416914565050438

https://www.facebook.com/profile.php?id=46687203018

https://www.facebook.com/profile.php?id=100003707548264&fref=ts

Bed Time Story TV Show https://www.facebook.com/profile.php?id=120382241399202

Twitter @

https://twitter.com/PWKidsBookshelf

https://twitter.com/OUPChildrens

https://twitter.com/childrens_book

https://twitter.com/ChildBookCircle

https://twitter.com/bleeschldrnsbks

https://twitter.com/Booksforchildrn

https://twitter.com/SFCMagazine

Radio Shows for Children:

http://www.kidspublicradio.org/lullaby.html

http://www.kidspublicradio.org/jabberwocky.html

http://www.kusp.org/

Pre-Order Campaign

Pre-order Campaigns are the most powerful way to launch a book and Smashwords offers great support and assistance with ebook pre-orders. Using this marketing tool, you can create interest in your book before it is published and customers are billed on the day when it is launched. Having all the sales on the release date will spike your book rank.

But, authors mustn't think that setting up a pre-order campaign means guaranteed success. Authors need to learn how to use pre-orders to get the best results. Timing is one of the most important factors in setting up such a campaign and it is recommended that you begin 4 to 6 weeks prior to the date when the book will be published. I want to convince you that making pre-orders is one more chance to increase your sales if you know how to make it work for you for your next book release.

Hit the Ebook Bestseller Lists with Preorders: A Guide to Pre-order Strategy from Smashwords, Inc.

I hope that you will find pre-ordering helpful and I would like to hear from you to know about the results of your pre-order campaign. Please go to the fan page of my book https://www.facebook.com/bookspromotion and leave a message. Tell me which publisher you used, for how long you ran it before the release day, how you promoted the pre-order campaign, and what the results were. To interest you in sharing your information with me, I am running a contest.

Share the cover of the book and this message: "Because of Madi Preda's book, *How to Promote and Market Your Book*, I sat up my preorder campaign with . . . for . . . weeks and promoted my book following her advice. Post the results on any social media platform, blog, or your website with a link to the book and you can be the lucky winner of a free month of publicity with Authors PR Madi Preda.

Send the link to me at authorspr@gmail.com with the word, contest, in the subject line. The winner will win the Spring Sales promotion for the month of March 2015.

If you make a blog post and share your success story with readers, I will share every single post sent to me on my blog http://authorspromotion.wordpress.com. Once again, this is more free publicity for every author. In order for me to share your post on my blog, please tell me in your message what you considered to be the most valuable piece of advice in this book, what you didn't like, and some of your personal experiences trying to promote your book in ways I've suggested.

How to Advertise a Pre-Order Campaign – Sample:

Pre-order campaign for . . . by . . . with great prizes for you to win.

Are you a fan reader of . . .? If not, read his/her latest novel . . . , which will be released in less than one month. State the theme of the book in one sentence such as: A tale of redemption, of finding answers and mentors in the most unexpected places.

We have a special offer going on for the release of . . . If you pre- order this book you can download his/her previous novel . . . for free.

Prizes and giveaways:

--All pre-orders will be delivered as autographed copies.

--Five lucky winners will receive a charm bracelet with lotus charms.

--One lucky reader will receive the grand prize. The other two books of this author, in paperback, will be autographed with a special dedication.

How to do it:

Look on Amazon (link here), pre-order, and email your proof of purchase to (email address). Don't forget to include your mail address (US only). You will get an email back when the items have been sent out.

Thank you and good luck.

Recommended for pre-order campaign:

Amazon, Book People, Smashwords, and of course the author's website.

How to generate sales for a new released book:

Advertising:

Many authors prefer to focus on with their writing and employ someone else to do the advertising for them. What if you decide to do it for yourself? If so, you have to step out from your cozy and safe place into the world of marketing in order to succeed.

Writing a book is quite different from writing content marketing, and to do this a writer must stretch and adapt, experiment, and take risks. It will take some time to discover what and how to successfully add information about your book to the market place. Talk to booksellers and librarians; visit successful authors' websites and forums to find out what is selling and what is not. You have to come up with something that readers want and enjoy. For this you need to exploit the strong points of your book and your strengths as a writer.

The first steps in advertising require that you write a synopsis of your book and a press release. Everyone will ask for these.

Synopsis:

Let us figure out how to write a synopsis, a useful tool in advertising your book.

The synopsis on the back cover should be short—maybe one paragraph or two at the most. You will need an extended one, under two pages, or even better, material that is concentrated on one single page, which will be sent with a cover letter to media outlets, radio, or TV shows.

1. Describe the relevance of the characters.

2. Present the most important scenes with an emphasis on the main character and offer specific scenes for the turning point, describing what happens and why.

3. Include information about characters' goals and motivations.

4. Raise questions and offer answers to keep the reader interested in reading your synopsis.

5. Include a resolution of the story with an ending that touches on all the story highlights.

6. Describe the main character's ultimate choice.

The synopsis must have a beginning, middle, and end. Without giving away too many details that might spoil the suspense, you must include the ending of the story for you are the one who know how the story ends.

Press releases:

I have heard from reputable sources that many journalists have their filters set up for the words, Press Release, so they are rejected from the start, being considered "fake news." However, people still keep sending them. It is not painful, and there are many sites that offer free services for sending press releases.

A press release is a written for the media. It can announce news about a book, including book signing events, where you want to invite media, website promotions, awards, accomplishments, or a fundraising campaign from the sales of your book.

How to write an eye-catching press release:

Write a genuine headline, brief, clear, and very representative for your book, character, or subject.

Write the body of the press release according to what you like to read in a news story. Some journalists might pick up on your press release, so what you write will be what they use in their column. Therefore, write your press release with the exact details about your book or event that you want to see in print.

- Start with the date, time, and place.

- The first sentence should catch the reader's attention and state briefly what is happening. This sentence expands the headline, provides some details, and takes the reader more fully into the story.

- The body content must elaborate on the first sentence. If the start of your press release generates interest then you have created the readers' attention.

- The best method for writing an effective press release is to keep in mind the following questions: Who, what, when, where, why, and how.

- Boilerplate: More about the author: Who are you? What are your achievements? What is your goal?

- Contact information:

Signal the end of the press release with three # (hash) symbols. This is a standard way of ending the press release.

A standard book press release template:

Contact Information:

Author and/or Publisher

Contact person and his/her info

Headline

Publisher and/or Author Announces the Release of **Title of Book and genre**

FOR IMMEDIATE RELEASE

City, State, **Publisher, and/or Author** are proud to offer the **latest, debut, etc.** work from **Author**, **Title of Book**, hitting bookstores everywhere on **Date**.

Book title is a **compelling tale, informative how-to, etc**, focused on **basic themes of book, or subject matter covered, if it's non-fiction**.

Expand the synopsis of the book and/or details about the author and the major point of the book that will make readers unable to resist buying it.

Quotes from author and/or any critics who have received upfront copies of the book.

Boilerplate about author and/or publisher.

Contact Information for Author and/or Publisher

Promotion

In order to generate sales you have to keep promoting. This will be always part of your lifestyle as a writer.

--Talk about your book everywhere you have the chance to do it.

--Hand out brochures, flyers, business cards, and bookmarks.

--Schedule a certain amount of time each day for promotion.

-Try to find new and original ideas for your promotional activity.

--Write sales pitches and post them everywhere and every time you can on different networks.

--Keep in touch with other writers and find out what kind of promotion works best in their case.

--Join online marketing seminars or hire a marketing consultant.

As a writer, you need to understand that in order to generate sales you have to be noticed. This is how you get exposure. Make speaking engagements, participate in writer's conferences, join writing groups, and reader/writer associations. Attend book signings and book fairs. Don't forget the easiest way—networking.

Network and Social Media: Network, network, network!

You need time to write and you want to devote yourself to doing this, but you have a book to sell so figure out the best use of your time and energy. Have a look at the social media channels. Take it one by one. Become familiarized with how they work. Choose a few that you like and develop your presence on these. From my experience, I have had good results with Reddit, StumbleUpon, and Pinterest for business. Don't forget Facebook and Twitter.

You can find a brief mention about a successful tweet campaign is an interview with the author of **"A Luminous Future"** – **Teodor Flonta,** which was retweeted more than 700 times. This is an example of how interviews help to sell books.

Another successful example of networking is: **Saving Our Pennies by Roy Dimond and Jeff Leitch.** As a result of social media networking, this book was in the top 100 bestsellers on Amazon in three categories in the first two weeks after the release date.

Judas Goat: The Kennet Narrow Boat Mystery by Patrick Brigham was featured on Facebook groups for kindle promotion and its rank was raised from 1.4 million to 56.000.

Find the Right Audience/Social Marketing/Content Marketing and Direct Marketing

Tips for Networking and Social Media

--Create editorial content that satisfies readers' needs.

--Develop a distribution strategy across web, social media, mobile, and emerging platforms. https://copromote.com/ offers incredible opportunities for instant social sharing on many platforms.

--Use different content types to reach your readers, including videos, audio, graphics, polls and surveys.

--Analyze content performances across the web http://whotalking.com. Here you can see your exposure on Twitter, Facebook, Blogs, Forums, Fickr, Google+ and You Tube.

--Comment on other people posts and share their content.

--Reciprocating link submission is another way to gain exposure.

--Build back links.

--Submit your site or blog to search engines and directories.

The key to the successful development of your author's brand are the major elements necessary for any brand building: Storytelling, Community, and Originality.

Storytelling: Everyone has a story to tell—so tell your story. Talk about your first try at writing—the big achievement of your poem being published in your school magazine. Gradually describe your work as an adult, mentioning articles in newspapers and magazines, or the journey of writing your new/latest book.

Share: Share with your readers how you started to write. They are human just as you are so tell them about your worries and fears about how your book will be received. Tell them about your hopes and how writing this book influenced your personal life. You don't have to pretend to be a brilliant writer who can write blind, with no worries and no feelings, that you knew from the very beginning that you would be successful. Be confident but not arrogant. Try to be funny. Honestly, readers are more inclined to like you if they realize that you are a normal person, not a green, big mouth academician from space. You could write a "How I start my Novel" post and share it through other social platforms.

I said from the beginning that this book is based on my own experience, so as an example, I want to share with you two funny stories. Like any other beginner, I hardly had any clients and I wanted to be successful. I wanted to promote authors.

One of the first authors I could work with said to me, "Hello, I am the best author in this genre and you will never read anything better than my books". When I asked him if he ever happened to be modest, he told me that he was modest only on Sundays. I decided that he wasn't the kind of author I wanted to work with, said goodbye, and left to talk with some other authors, not so famous, but modest all the time. ☺

The other story involves an offer I wrote that I was accepting barter deals, thinking that someone could develop my website for me or pay me with a subscription to a literary association that I would like to join. A writer responded by asking if he should pay me in chickens and goats. Why goats? Maybe because I live in Greece.

I tell you these stories in the hope that you, my readers, will be nice and friendly when you respond to a request or an offer, treat everyone with kindness and don't treat anybody like you are one step ahead.

Even better, let your community tells your brand story and this will help you to make the step ahead. This will help your advertising and marketing efforts.

Community: You probably have a community already but perhaps you haven't thought about it. Your religious community, your friends and neighbors, your colleagues—are connected to their communities in a variety of ways. Reach out to all of them. Let them know about your book or your event (book signings, speaking engagements, library presentations).

They can recommend you to their friends and colleagues. They can suggest new contacts for you or post information about you on their social media platforms. The process is like a squid, with tentacles spreading in different communities of yours, your friends, and the friends of friends. You can't know ahead of time how many people you might reach in this but if you are making a career as a writer, be transparent about it and engage your community. You can do this through social media and you can do it real life. Talk with people. Ask for advice and recommendations. Usually they will help if they can. Do you think you don't have enough time or patience to do all these? Then think about finding someone who will do it for you. Choose carefully and chose wisely.

Originality. A successful brand is the one that presents you as you really are, across all platforms and networks. Don't present yourself or your books as similar to such and such a writer because they are successful. Instead, if you mention that your book is similar to a particular author that the reader knows, find a way to talk about your book in a way that intrigues the reader. Introduce yourself and your book as having something new and unique to offer, something that defines you and your writing style.

Do you really need a publicist? What a good publicist can do: The role of a publicist is to build and promote a good public image, to create a reputation for the author, and expose the books to media and readers. The way to create exposure is to create a message that resonates with the targeted market. At Authors PR I like to build and cultivate a relationship with our writers and our readers in a variety of ways, each plan tailored to the specific author.

What to do and what not to do when you approach a publicist: Don't tell too many hard luck stories. You can discuss these in private emails but the role of a publicist is to say how good you are, not to make people feel sorry for you.

When writing your bio, forget this: I live with three dogs and two cats. Okay, this might say you are a good person and you love animals, but nobody is that interested in how many pets you have.

Don't forget to share posts of other people who write about you and your books on your website and in social media. The publicist has spent time finding people willing to publish a promotional spot for you so always send them a thank you note.

When you send the usual information to your publicist (synopsis, bio, or answers to interview questions) create new and interesting content. There is no point publicizing the same information currently available on Amazon or your publisher's site. If readers are interested in your book, they expect to find something new about your book.

What to keep in mind:

Your publicist is part of your team. My motto is: **"Don't hire me. Invite me to be part of your team and your success."**

20 Steps to gain exposure for your book:

1. What is the purpose of your marketing plan?

--Are you promoting your last book, all of your books, your website, or are you promoting a book that is free for a certain period of time?

2. Timing

--For how long are you ready to run this campaign?

--Is there a specific launch time?

--Are there distinct periods of time such as: seasonal, holiday, special event?

3. Budget and costs

--What budget do you have for paid advertising/PR/Marketing?

--Can you support other costs such as: printing promotional materials, launch parties, travelling?

4. Publicity and PR

--Set up a press kit with audio and video links, including press clippings and articles.

--Have teasers that catch the attention of readers and viewers.

5. Contact Local Media

--Play the "local writer" and contact local newspapers, magazines and radio local stations.

6. Contact National Media

--Send press releases that target cities and subject related magazines.

7. Book Reviewers

--Send review copies for reviewers in various publications. Be aware of time frames and reviewer's requirements.

--Send review copies to book clubs and community groups, targeting your genre.

8. Articles

--Write and submit articles to the print media about the book, about the subject, about you as a writer, even about your writing process.

9. Speaking engagements

--Make an offer to speak at your local library, schools, and local organizations and associations where your book could have an impact.

--If your book focuses on a specific age group, visit appropriate groups such as senior centers and homes, children's nurseries, playgrounds, party venues for children.

--Keep an eye out for competitions where your books might be offered as a prize or gift.

10. Networking

--Join a few social media channels and try to be as active as you can. This is a good way to build your brand and reputation online as an author.

11. Launch your book in local bookstores

--Send press releases for the event to local media, reading groups, local librarians.

--Send invitations to friends.

--Send a thank you note to every person who attended the event.

--Donate a few books to your local library.

12. Promotional materials

--Make business cards and bookmarks with the cover and a description of your story, your website, and if you have one, your free eBook.

--Create a promotional business card for books you will sell for a special price if you have written other books.

--Spread the business cards out. Offer them to libraries, bookstores, office supplier shops, hotels, local supermarket or any other places you can think off.

13. Word-of mouth

--This is a very important way to advertise your book. Consider family, friends, colleagues, and neighbors. If you strike up a conversation in a store or on a bus or train, offer the person a bookmark or a business card. If you have set up your website so readers can read excerpts of your books, let people know.

--Be sure you have a share button on your website.

14. Advertising

--Do it by target: by location (place of birth, place of living, where the action in your book takes place), by subject and social issues, and, if the by genre and interests.

15. Co-Promotion

--Target authors of the same genre for reviews, guest blogging, and co-promotion.

16. Cross Promotion

--A book about meditation in nature or healthy lifestyle could be advertise or sold in campsite shops, gyms, health food stores, shops selling sports accessories and clothes—even some health practitioners' offices.

--A book on the history of a country might be proposed for university courses about the history of this country.

--A diet book can be promoted at your local gym, fitness club, or health food store.

17. Charity

--Consider donating a part of your book sales to a charity that is important to you. Giving even a small percentage of your sales to a non-profit organization could make a huge difference in people's lives. Your book will gain exposure and you will feel good about doing a kind act (only if you are that kind of person who cares).

18. Short Stories Anthology

--Contribute with a short story to an anthology related to the subject in your book and you will be mentioned with your book in the resource box.

19. Blogs and Bloggers

--Be in touch with bloggers who review books, for interviews, for guest posts.

--Organize a blog tour for yourself or ask a blogger who does this to do it for you.

--Ask for a cover reveal.

--Ask for a promotional spot for your launching event, your book, or a public appearance

20. If all of the above seems too much or too hard for you this problem can be easily solved. FIND A PUBLICIST!

How to Sell More Books by Reaching the Right Audience for Your Book

When you are considering the best way to reach your audience you have to analyze who your audience is and then use this information to plan strategy, style, promotional materials and visual presentation. Different audiences have different needs.

Demographic factors

--Age, gender, religion, education level, income, and location. Does your book focus on a particular age group? People's priorities, and perspectives tend to change as they age so you need to shape the description of your book to attract the age range of readers that you want to target.

--Gender is just as important as religion. In the beginning, if you don't choose the right audience to market your book it has little or no chance of succeeding.

--Education level and income play a role in the buying habits of your readers. You have to keep in mind these factors when you plan your marketing campaign.

Personality

Understanding the target reader's personality will help to make the message of the book more effective. Knowing your audience is the key to marketing success. In order to identify personality preferences of your readers you have to keep in mind the four basic dimensions of your book's characters:

-Introvert -extrovert

-Sensing-intuitive

-Thinking-feeling

-Judging-perceiving

The secret in developing effective market strategies is to find your characters' strengths and give readers logical reasons for reading your book. When writing promotional material keep in mind these different aspects of personality. This could increase the number of readers who want to buy your book.

Values and beliefs

Here the analysis is focused on values and beliefs, goals and lifestyles. Find out what is important for your readers and then you will find it easier to organize the information about the book in a way that seems natural and real to your readers, even if it is a work of fiction.

Building effective messages

What you really want when marketing your book is to match readers' habits with their environment so you have the opportunity to influence their reading attitude and choices.

You can do this by finding uniform groupings that are keen on the same subject or settings as in your book.

People's culture is defined by their values, philosophies, and attitudes, and reveals itself in their myths, heroes, and stories or in the allocation of space.

Writing, Speaking, and Visual Message:

Written messages make it easy to:

--Present specific details of the book subject and characters.

--Present an extensive and complex biography of the author.

--Communicate a message that is designed to affect readers emotions.

Speaking in public is more efficient if you want to:

--Answer questions.

--Use emotions to persuade readers to buy your book.

--Provoke an immediate response or action to your writing.

--Focus the readers' attention on specific points.

Meeting with readers clubs, community groups, and making oral presentation in libraries or bookshops are important ways of reaching the audience.

Book Trailers and Short video clips are important for the visual impact of your message:

You can make them as an advert clip, a documentary, or even as a cartoon. Create something that you think will catch readers' attention. In order to make a book trailer you can chose to pay someone who can do it for you or do it yourself, for little or no money.

Try out: Windows Media Player, Animoto, Vimeo, Stupeflix. There are many choices.

1. Write a few teasers about the book, the story, and the characters.

2. Find and download images to match the teasers that you can find on PublicDomain.Net, MorgueFile, Pixabay, iStockPhoto.

3. Import the pictures into your moviemaker program. Add the teasers for each picture. Then format. Almost all moviemakers give you some choices regarding fonts, transition effects, or where to add the text. The time recommendation for a book trailer is between two and three minutes. If you want to add music to your trailer, try SoundSnap.com or other royalty free music sites.

4. Upload your video to You Tube or other sites that suit your marketing choice and share it everywhere. If you have an electronic newsletter, include your video.

Virtual book tours and how they can help:

If you have the possibility to do book signings at a local bookstore or library, do so. Some people consider that old fashion and time consuming, so more authors prefer to reach their audience through a virtual book tour, for a cover reveal, or for launching their books on social media. A virtual book tour is a great way to sell books, to let people know about your book, and gives you a chance to grow your mailing list.

A virtual book tour involves posts about you and your book on several blogs. Some of the bloggers will want to review your book, interview you, and post excerpts from the book or video clips on their blogs. You have an opportunity to appear in front of a wider audience. Just think of 20 blog hops, each having 400 followers, which means 800 people will read and take notice of your book and your brand. Be sure you provide links as to where and how people can buy the book, links to your website or blog, and your social media platforms. Ask them to get in touch with you through email and subscribe to your email list. If you create a Google spreadsheet for sign-ups you will have their email address. When you send the blogger a thank you note for helping you, ask them if they would like to be informed about any new release, review your soon to be published new book or host the next blog tour for you.

Make bloggers feel special. Share their post on your social media platforms. Tell them how helpful they were. You can offer an Amazon gift or coupon, a paperback autographed copy, a poster to download with thanks for participation.

It works in the same way for cover reveals.

Here is a sample of a sign-up form for a blog tour

https://docs.google.com/forms/
d/14iITHMaup5HWtOVGySZq90hvhSEQpZmp5VrnA_ooUc4/viewform

Blogging

Connect with people worldwide.

Blogging helps us to network with people across the world, whether they are writers, readers, or people who share the same hobby. Being in contact with people from different countries and cultures may help you to understand your audience better, and may help you acquire more fans. It will definitely help you to spread the word about your magnificent book. As you know, word of mouth is an effective way of advertising your book.

In my case, since I started to write my blog, I've improved my writing skills and style as English is not my first language. I was afraid that I would be criticized if I made a mistake. I made a lot. Still do. ☺ This fear was the engine that motivated me to improve my writing skills.

Once anyone becomes a blogger, he or she may become interested in several other aspects related to blogging that will help them to improve their own blog. For example, I was never interested in graphic design. After I started blogging, I developed the motivation to create eye-catching newsletters, posters, and other promotional materials for authors. Later on my interest grew to include making short video clips and book trailers, even book covers.

Blogs promote your business. An author should treat his/her book as a business

Blogs play an important role in the promotion of any kind of product or business. The blog acts as a platform for displaying the books you want to sell. Once you have created a blog it is easy to share content with social media sites like Facebook, Twitter, LinkedIn, Google Plus, Pinterest, and Instagram, so this is a good way to get exposure and keep in touch with your audience online.

Some specialized blogs are valuable sources of information for writers and you can gain information related to the technical aspects of writing, publishing, marketing, and promoting by visiting them regularly.

There are millions of blogs in the blogosphere and you have to look for ones that are interesting to you as an author. Look for other writers' blogs, readers, and reviewers. Follow them. Read their posts and make comments. Share and like and they will follow you back and become your audience.

In a way, a blog may represent your portfolio. Here you can you share your books, your articles, and your thoughts so the audience gets to know you. Blogging is an excellent platform to showcase your brand.

Many writers, even if they gain a certain level of reputation, still run an online blog as additional support. Blogs help you to get more exposure and create fan pages in social media. When your blog starts to have more followers, you achieve more popularity.

If a writer doesn't feel confident speaking in public then of course he can't do radio interviews or TV shows. Creating a blog might be a good way to develop self-confidence in one's ability as a writer and could help to decrease the power of this phobia when dealing with the public.

Continue your blogging journey with enthusiasm. If you create engaging content and an interesting call to action, you will be pleased with the results.

Tips To Attract Readers:

--Interesting and useful content on your blog makes visitors not only to want read it, but also to share the post.

--Use social media to find new readers—people who share your interests.

--Post articles that are relevant to your target audience.

--Create smart headlines to attract readers.

--Keywords are necessary to attract readers- search your genre, readers clubs, books reviewers, book bloggers.

--Make some posts before you publish your book. Ask for feedback on the cover and the most important chapter. Ask for opinions about the main character.

--Use the blog to create interest and try to gain buyers for your book. Post announcements about giveaway, contests. Offer little prizes.

How to gain more readers for your blog by interviewing other authors

When you interview other authors you gain exposure to new audiences—their audience become yours because they share the interview with their social media platform and they have their own followers. All you have to do is to find possible guests and/or other authors of books in the same genre as yours. This way the interview will be more interesting because you know what to ask and you have experience with this specific topic.

How to find authors? They are everywhere, Amazon, GoodReads, Facebook . . . Just ask if they would like to be interviewed by you for your blog, which covers a similar topic and that you are an author of the same genre.

How do you make it simple and not very time consuming? The easiest way to do this is to create a page on your blog only for interviews. This way you can have a set of standard questions, a submission guideline, and a form to send it.

I like to personalize every interview, focusing on the book, yet finding out about the author. I think every book and every author are unique and must be treated accordingly. Making an effort to read about the person you want to interview as well as his/her book is a way of showing respect and consideration for the author. This is also a good recommendation for you, as a person because you are doing the interview with dedication, not just writing superficially in order to have regular posts. In doing this, you will be treated similarly.

Offer to review other authors' books and post your review together with a little promotional spot—a few words about author and the book, links to author's social media and also related articles and blog posts. This gives you a chance to connect with other authors. Since they have the same chance it is a win-win situation.

Lynn Worton – Blogger and Reviewer

My Experience as a Reviewer

My love of the English language and reading started at school. I had a wonderful teacher who encouraged me to read and spell words correctly, and put them in the correct context in a sentence. I was not a fast reader by any means when I began (as most children aren't aged 6 or 7), but I started to get better.

The school librarian was a big influence in my life. She introduced me to different authors and genres, and encouraged me to keep trying until I found a book that I enjoyed. I remember the first book that caught and held my attention; it was a children's edition of Pride and Prejudice by Jane Austin. I then began to read books by Enid Blyton, as well as Nancy Drew and The Hardy Boy's series (by Terry Munson and Franklin W. Dixon respectively). This cemented my love of reading. Then, as I grew older and hit puberty, I began to read Mills and Boon romances, as well as science fiction and fantasy novels. As my love for reading increased, so did the thirst for more and more books in different genres. My vocabulary increased, my spelling got better and my reading speed got faster. By the time I left high school, I was reading two Mills and Boon stories a day.

I first started out reviewing books as an admin on a Facebook page in January 2012, after being offered the opportunity from the page owner in a contest; I am still an admin on her page today. After about six months of administrating, I then decided to make my own page, when I found out that I actually enjoyed doing it. I began Book Reviews by Lynn on Facebook in June of 2012. I then opened a blog page by the name of Book Reviews by Lynn in March 2013. I offer book reviews, promos, interviews, blog tours and giveaways; as well as anything else that I think people would be interested in. I write honest reviews from the heart; if I like a book, I will say so. Conversely, if I do not like the story, I will also say so. Luckily, I haven't come across that many that I don't like! I focus my reviews mostly on the characters, the flow of the story and how it made me feel.

It has not been an easy few years, but it has been very rewarding. I have read some amazing books, and in genres that I would never have had a chance to do so normally. The demand for reviews by authors in the wake of the opening of the self-publishing industry, and the availability of e-readers, has kept me busy. Unfortunately, this demand has created a problem for reviewers such as myself. There are only so many hours in the day, and trying to find time to read whilst juggling a job, home and family, not to mention keeping up a social media presence, can cause a bottleneck in the ability to read as many books as one would like; it does help if you are a fast reader such as myself, but it is not a prerequisite.

An author has an expectation that their book will be read within a few days or weeks after handing them over to a reviewer. But, when a reviewer has several authors clamoring for reviews, this may not always be possible. I try to read the books on my reviewing list as fast as I can, but even so, it is still slow progress. It is amazing how quickly a list can go from one to over five hundred books strong! It took me roughly three months to reach that figure, and I am still struggling to get below the four hundred mark nearly eighteen months later.

The one thing I do actually hate is being sent a book by an author who does not take the time to read my review preferences. I have been sent books in genres that I do not read. This is not necessarily a bad thing, as I have tried a few and enjoyed them. But, when the authors send books without checking with me first, this really upsets me. I know a few of my blogger friends have the same problem. In general, the authors are very understanding and patient about the time delay, but there are a few that get impatient. I do not blame them; I can understand their desire to find out what a reader thinks of their hard work.

However, authors need to learn to contact reviewers or bloggers first before sending out their books, read their reviewing policies and be patient. A bit of common courtesy from both authors and reviewers never hurts either and, it would help avoid any unnecessary unpleasantness for all concerned; there is no call for bad manners. I treat everyone, not just authors, with respect and I expect the same from the people who deal with me.

I have not had any bad experiences with authors, apart for them sending books without checking with me, but I have a few blogger friends who have fallen foul of abuse. Unfortunately, this also applies to authors I know. They too have fallen foul of abuse by readers or bloggers, and are publicly bullied on the major social media sites.

In this highly technological age, this means that reputations are made and ruined in the stroke of a few buttons on a keyboard. This cyber bullying is a major issue that needs to be addressed. Bullying is wrong, whether on the playing field, in the home or in cyber space. Unfortunately, it is very difficult to police the bullies in cyber space, as they hide behind avatars and fake usernames. Most bullies are frustrated and jealous of another's success (no matter which profession), and have serious self-esteem issues. They too may have been bullied at one time or another, and the saying "Misery loves company" is all too true. Another true saying, "The pen is mightier than the sword", also gives bullies a weapon. Words can be used to help or harm, depending on the context and the way they are interpreted. An innocent sentence in a review (in the eyes of the reviewer) can be construed to be a personal attack on the author. Or, it could be an outright personal attack on the author by the reader/reviewer for something the author wrote in the story that the reader didn't like. In either case, this is not helpful to either party. Constructive criticism on a book is always welcome by an author, as it helps them hone their skills. If the grammar is in need of re-editing, or there is a problem with the continuity and flow, I always send an e-mail (when possible) to the author. However, I generally try not to mention these issues in a review. This is one way that stops the author feeling like I am publically raking them over the coals. No one, authors included, wants their work to be publicly humiliated. If an executive in a top company had the same scrutiny on their work, would they cope? I don't think so. Some things should remain private in my opinion. A fair grasp of the English language (or which ever language the book is written in), spelling and grammar also helps when reading/reviewing, but again, not altogether important. However, the reader needs to be able to read and understand what the author is trying to say. Authors also have to watch out for spelling mistakes and the difference between US English and UK English.

I am a bit of a stickler for correct grammar and spelling in a book as a reader, as obvious errors break the flow of the story, but I can overlook the occasional typo; we are only human and we all make mistakes. However this can, and has, caused several problems between authors and readers.

I have mostly worked with, and read books by, independent authors since beginning my reviewing "career". However, I have also read books that have been released from the mainstream publishing houses. There is not a lot of difference between "indie" and "mainstream" apart from the editing, formatting and marketing, in my opinion. Granted, the mainstream publishers have the contacts and experience to get books marketed and distributed to bookstores and libraries around the world. But, indie authors have the freedom to write and publish what they want, without being categorized into pigeon holes. There is scope to mix several genres into a compelling story. Today, there are many different genres and sub-genres to choose from that never existed five years ago. I love to read these mixed genres, as they give the author a chance to think outside of the box, and the reader the chance to experience a full range of emotions whilst journeying to some amazing places without leaving the comfort of their chair or bed. I know of an indie author who was trying to write a contemporary, sweet romance, but her characters wouldn't cooperate. She struggled for weeks to get her characters to behave, but they wanted the story to flow in a different direction. Her book is now an older young adult, paranormal romance, and I am looking forward to reading it soon.

I love reading, and I hope to keep reading and reviewing for many years to come. I was not expecting my life to change so drastically when I first accepted that offer to admin on a Facebook page, but now it has. I am exceedingly grateful for the opportunity to share my passion of reading with the people of the world. If someone offers you the opportunity to share your passion (whatever it may be), I suggest you grab it with both hands! It is one of the most rewarding things I have done, and I have made new friends with the same passion as myself.

Speaking of rewarding, I have also been involved in crowdfunding books. This is a relatively new way for authors to get the necessary funds together to have their books published. Crowdfunding is not just for authors though. It can be used for other businesses and projects that would not necessarily be funded by a bank or other financial institutions. There are several different types of crowdfunding platforms and events, depending on the required funding. Books and publications are usually crowdfunded through a rewards based system. I have funded a few books in this way, and have signed copies of the books sitting on my bookshelf. The biggest platforms for this are Indiegogo and Kickstarter. However, there are several other platforms to choose from.

If you want to repay the authors for all their hard work, the biggest compliment you can give them is a review – whether short or long, in favour or against. There is no right or wrong way to write a review, but always write from the heart, and explain why the book touched you enough to write the review. This is what I have learnt in the last few years. Make your words mean something to both the author of the book, and the readers who would be interested in reading the story themselves. Try not to put in "spoilers", as there is nothing worse than reading a review with "He did this.", "She said that." and "This is what happened." in them. This puts off potential readers faster than you can say "Allegiant by Veronica Roth". The hubbub about that particular book has ruined it for thousands of readers, myself included. However, I am still looking forward to reading the book, as I have avoided reading any of the reviews; I prefer to find out the story in my own way, rather than being told exactly what happens. Most of the readers and bloggers I know are of the same mind. Reading is not only a hobby to me; it is a passion and obsession. I encourage everyone to pick up a book, an e-reader or an audio copy. If there were no authors or books, the world would be a lot bleaker and extremely boring in my opinion. There have been storytellers since the dawn of man, and it would be a shame if this art form became extinct. Stories can be educational, informative and entertaining. Pick up a book, no matter the subject, and get swept away in it (although, I'm not sure if a Text Book counts except to the academic!). Go on, I dare you!

I am hoping to expand into offering a Proofreading and Editing service in the future, and I am in the process of enrolling in a course to enable me to do so. I am feeling a bit nervous, but hopeful. This would be a dream come true for me. In the meantime, I will continue to read and review as many books as I can, for as long as I can.

You can contact me on the following links:

Book Reviews by Lynn on Facebook https://www.facebook.com/BookReviewsByLynn

Twitter handle: @LynnWorton or https://twitter.com/LynnWorton Hash tags: #lynnworton #bookreviewsbylynn

Blog: Book Reviews by Lynn http://bookreviewsbylynn.blogspot.co.uk/

LinkedIn: https://www.linkedin.com/profile/view?id=208901072&trk=nav_responsive_tab_profile_pic

Booklikes: http://notrow1.booklikes.com/

Amazon US Reviewer Profile: http://www.amazon.com/gp/pdp/profile/A2K5MN1OE6UPXF

Amazon UK Reviewer Profile: https://www.amazon.co.uk/gp/pdp/profile/A2K5MN1OE6UPXF?ie=UTF8&ref_=ya_your_profile

How to use Twitter to promote Your Book

When you start tweeting, keep in mind that you want to bring your message in front of the right people. Tweet in an effective manner. Target your audience by keywords, interest, and location.

Write short messages—140 characters, or even less, and bring it to the target audience by including their @username in the body of your tweet. The message should be written as if you are having a conversation with your readers, in a friendly and approachable style.

What you say and how you say it will affect how they react and communicate with you. People respond to friendly tweets; don't be overly formal.

You must not forget the five **W's** of marketing, **Who, What, When, Where,** and **Why** and the major goals to remember when you compose your tweets:

Who -- establish and increase your brand and drive web traffic to your blog or website.

What -- launch your new book, website, blog or fan page, announce an event, describe what is what.

When – release date of the book and when the event takes place.

Where -- provide the links for book, website, blog, fan page, or the location for your event.

Why –cover reveal, launch the book, asking for reviews, blog tour

Tools to make your tweets appear in search engines results

Use keywords that best describe your genre, your writing style, location, the main character, or the settings of your book and use # hashtags to group your tweets with others on the similar topics.

Hashtags: #deal, #bargain, #coupon, #giveaway, #contest, #free, #jointheteam, #reviews #blogtour, #shoutout, #RT #indietribe #writersdream.

@bkmkting @IndieAuthorNews @businesstweetpr @TheLitSyndicate @indieboundbooks @AuthorShout @Editorial_Indie @SimplePromote

Twitter Tips. Use **Buffer** https://bufferapp.com/app/ to set up automatic tweets; this way you don't have to worry about and spending your day tweeting.

How to use Pinterest to promote your Book

Pinterest is another social media platform that can generate traffic to your blog or website and help you get exposure for your books as well as drive sales. All the statistics say that in the last year Pinterest gained a huge number of users and audience. I really think it's worth our marketing time.

Get a Business Pinterest Account at http://business.pinterest.com and start pinning by creating a board on a specific topic about your book and your writing, to attract followers. Use the same keywords that you already use for your blog, your website or your tweets.

Like and comment on other people pins with the same interests, and they will go to see what are you pinning about. You can follow a specific board or a user account.

You can pin posts from other social media platforms, your own or others, or you can share your blog posts. This way you generate traffic because every pin will include the link back to your blog post.

Think about launching a Pinterest contest and write a blog post to promote it in such a way that engages and calls to action. Ask the users to create a pinboard on their own account and boards and say why they like your book. Ask them to send you the link so that you can track all the participants. Let users know that the best board will win a free book, paperback or electronic edition.

On Pinterest you can share offline events as well and let people know about when and where you are doing a book signing or a radio interview. Ask them to join by pinning on boards targeted by location.

Tips for creating boards:

- By genre: and invite other authors to join

- By geography: British authors, US authors, Canadian authors, in concordance with your location

- By subject: WW II authors, diet books, bullying book, psychology, alternative medicine, forgotten culture, etc.

- By giveaways: and invite other authors to post on your board

Once again, **think outside the box** to find new strategies for your promotion.

How to Use Facebook for advertising

Facebook is another network platform where you can advertise your book. You can create a fan page and post all the announcements about the book. Begin with a pre-order book campaign and the release date, and then continue with your promotion. Share the latest news, interviews, book tour, short video clips and everything you can think of that will attract your readers and engage your target audience.

Facebook has a few apps that are very helpful for authors:

Fan Appz — creates polls, quizzes, promotions, coupons and many other things.

Later Bro — is an app that gives you the possibility to schedule a post for later on.

Meeting Room — lets you conduct a live face-to-face meeting with your fans.

Go to http://apps.facebook.com/authorapp/ and there is another app, **Read my Book** or you can have a **Newsletter sign – up** on your fan page.

There are paid Facebook ads as well if you would like to spend some money on this.

As with all the other social media platforms, you not only gain fans and exposure for your book, you gain friends by creating contacts with people who share your passion, the love for written words.

LinkedIn Marketing Solutions

Social Selling with LinkedIn

Social selling helps to develop your own professional brand and social network, to gather insights and connections, and then enables you to use that information to discover new opportunities.

Social selling is transforming the traditional sales process of sales lead generation, sales prospecting, cold calling, building, and maintaining relationships, and much more.

LinkedIn's sales offer tools.

Reach new audiences

Professional audience – LinkedIn offers a large audience of active and professional influencers that help with brand awareness, building relationships, and connecting with people interested in your area of interest

Precision targeting – helps to indentify the right audience with individualized searches by job title and function, industry or company size.

You can set up your own budget and you can stop your ads anytime. There are no long-term contracts.

LinkedIn offers a variety of ad formats:

- -text and image ads
- -text only ads
- -video ads

Websites and Media Press Kit

Website for authors and books

Authors are the masters of words, but not many of them are very good on the Web. No blame at all, you can't be the best in everything, but you can try to do your best. Times are changing and more modern authors realize the importance of having a good website that allows them to connect their work with media, readers and other authors.

Every book is different and every author has his/her own style. Therefore, having a website is like a puzzle with many different pieces. You have to find the piece that fits perfectly in order to solve the puzzle, which is creating an effective website that will encourage people to learn more about you and your work.

How can you do this? Look at other authors' web sites to see their concepts, but yours must be tailored to your style and to your book, even though there might be aspects that are similar.

Home Page

The first thing to do when you create your website is the **Home Page**, the most important page of the entire site. Here you include a professional headshot, a biography, and your work email address if you don't mind making it public. If you do, you need a contact form. If you a have a radio interview, or a podcast, that describes you and your writing, here is the place to embed it. On this page you can talk about why you write this genre of books, what you love about it, and something about who you are and what you like.

On the landing page I recommend having announcements about up-coming events such as book signings, (when and where), speaking engagements, give away campaigns, (free or reduced price).

It's a good idea is to promote your work in progress or future projects, including some "behind the covers" blurb, a work cover if you have one, and the presumptive date of release.

Next page- **Published Books**

Include other titles. If you have too many or intend to, then set up a page for each of them or just make a list with these titles linked to any retailer where readers can see what the books are about. It is good to include thumbnails covers.

Interviews, book trailers, blog mentions, reviews, and press clips must be shared for each book. Include how and where they can be ordered, preferably not by saying "buy the book" but "it can be ordered by …" or click the cover to find out more, a less aggressive form of inviting your readers to buy it.

A Q&A for each book will give readers the possibility to go more deeply into the story. You can interest them in finding out more about the book by clicking on the cover.

Social Media Links: This is ideal if you can do it or ask your web master to link the website with some of your social media profiles or blog. Each page must have a button to share and like buttons for a few of the social media platforms.

Promotional Materials: Here you (and your website designer) get to be more creative by including a slideshow or a YouTube video, a quiz, or a poll, or other things that engage readers and tie into the content of your books. Sometimes authors are experts in their field and their books are an extension of a larger career. This is a great opportunity to include something interesting from the larger context of your career.

Contact Information: Many authors leave this for the last page but you want to make sure you have this information on the home page as well.

Here are two examples of sites I have worked on without having any kind of training in computers so you can do it as well.

http://roydimond.tripod.com and http://authorspr.tripod.com Have a look and keep in mind what I said at the beginning: You want to adapt your website to your needs.

Media Press Kit for Authors

Now, you have a website set up, a blog, and joined all the social media sites. Sure you have heard many times about the importance of having a press kit, but why is this so important? This media press kit is what you use when you approach newspapers, radio, magazines, libraries, and booksellers or communities. I see the media press kit as an expanded business card, which tells everything about the author and his/her books.

With a press kit in your hands, along with your book, you will sound more convincing. Your interlocutors will notice that you are professionally prepared, with portfolio in hand. A well thought out press kit sells. For online contacts set up a professional looking email and include your media press kit if you are asking for a book signing event, a radio interview, if you want your book to be featured by a magazine, or displayed in any venue.

Important tip: set up a signature for your email, it may be your website or blog or your fan page.

Reputable influencers in marketing suggest different materials to be assembled in this press kit but as a general rule you need to include all information in a clear and well-designed package. In this competitive book market, people are overwhelmed with authors trying to sell more and more books. It's wonderful to see so much talent out there and you can't make something much different from the others. So let's see what other authors put in their press kit.

Here is a basic list but feel free to adapt your kit to fit your needs and your style.

--Create a short biography as well as an extended one. Sometime you need to present what your interlocutor requires on the spot. Be efficient by having two alternatives of your biography readily available.

--A professional headshot or the best photo you have, not from twenty years ago when you were very charismatic. People want to see a current photo of the author.

--Start with one page. This is a page that is designed to give a description of you, your book, and a photo of your book cover. Be sure to include your email and website on this page. Put all the information on one page using a concise and tidy format. This is the shortest version, recommended especially for first time writers.

--For the extended version I recommend that you start with the longer biography on the first page. Then continue with your book description and your book cover on page two, including details of the product, ISBN number, publisher details, and available formats. If you have many books, make a page for each of them. On the next page select from the best reviews for each book and include a Q& A section. For this you need to provide a few questions that you would like to be asked, as well as their answers to give your interviewer some guidance. It also helps to list a few of your interviews and other public appearance or media clips.

--Lastly, I recommend that you include an excerpt for each book, the hot spot of the book, and if you have a work in progress include this or say something about future projects.

When you present yourself in a professional way, when you are prepared, many doors open.

Electronic Newsletter

This is a great way to spread the word about your book. When I began, I discovered this app to create electronic newsletters or flyers. For me it works the best and here you can see a sample https://www.smore.com/yvfc-the-purple-morrow .

This is the one that I have been using from the very beginning and continue to use it because it fits my needs as a marketer and will work for you as an author as well. It is easy to operate and offers many features such as:

--Offers style and design, custom backgrounds, and fonts.

--Lets you print and save your flyer as PDF or JPEG.

--Allows you to post it on Craigslist or embed on your website.

--Has a button that enables you to invite your Facebook friends and a share button for

Twitter, Pinterest, and Google.

--Allows you to email flyers, which I use to approach booksellers or even media outlets.

Something that I have found useful is the analytics, which gives you an overview, traffic sources, and email reports. You can see how many times people have looked at it, and, if they opened it, how much time they spent on it. This enables you to judge if they were interested or if they just dumped it. In addition, I simply love the map where you can see the map of your viewers, which gives me a smile every time I look at it. Seeing the map, getting red with flags from locations where you have sent the newsletter gives a feeling of "this is real." People everywhere are seeing the newsletter, which is great.

A great opportunity is that **SMORE** allows you to keep mailing lists and reuse them every time you want to send a newsletter for a book or for an event. You can also build your subscribers list and send them a monthly newsletter. They have a free and a paid version; the paid one has far more features.

How to improve book sales with distributors help

The best way to sell a book is through bookstores. How can you get your book into a book distributor warehouse? If you are published by a traditional publishing company, they will do it for you.

Independent book distributors are specialized companies, dealing with the distribution process. They work with smaller publishing companies and overseas publishing companies who wish to distribute their books to a new market in another country. The most important thing to say here is that distributors **work** with self-published authors. Of course, there are some criteria to be satisfied but it can be done.

You can contact as many bookstores as you like but you have to know that some of them deal only with book distributors. By having your book taken by a book distributor, you can then begin concentrating on writing your next book.

List of Independent Book Distributors:

Bella Distribution, http://www.belladistribution.com

BookMasters Distribution Services, http://www.bookmastersdistribution.com

Delphi Distribution, http://www.delphidistribution.com

Ingram Publisher Services, http://www.ingrampublisherservices.com.

National Book Network, http://www.nbnbooks.com http://www.nbnbooks.com/ProspectivePublisher/Index.shtml

NBN Kids, http://www.nbnbooks.com/NBNkids/index.shtml

New Leaf Distribution Services, http://www.newleaf-dist.com. Submission information: http://www.newleafvendors.com.

New Shelves Distribution, http://www.newshelvesdistribution.com.

Perseus Distribution Services, http://www.cdsbooks.com.

SCB Distributors, http://www.scbdistributors.com

Small Press Distribution, http://www.spdbooks.org

STL Distribution Services, http://www.stl-distribution.com

Charles E Tuttle Publishing, http://www.tuttlepublishing.com

30 Book Marketing Tips:

I have included a variety of tips and I am sure that you will find something on the to do list that you can do to build your brand and sell your book.

1. Create a testimonial page on your website.

2. Offer advanced reading copies ARC.

3. Ask fans to post their reviews on your Facebook page.

4. Ask fans to post their reviews on Amazon.

5. Ask fans to post their reviews on Goodreads.

6. Offer bloggers advanced reading copies.

7. Set up a virtual book tour.

8. Create your street team.

9. Create seasonal videos: Mother's day book, Summer Reads, Have Fun in the Sun, Autumn fall, Santa's Book Recommendation, Spring-new reads, etc.

10. Register as an author on Amazon, Goodreads, AuthorsDen, Google Authorship.

11. Create a book trailer and short video clips.

12. Use key words, hashtags, and smart teasers for every single post.

13. Post a blog post as often as you can, not only about your book, but also include information about your work and offer support to others.

14. Write articles and short stories and publish them online.

15. Join writers' conferences and writing contests.

16. Use Google, Pinterest, and Facebook Campaigns to get traffic for your website or blog and to gain more fans.

17. Create a newsletter and share the latest news with your subscribers.

18. Write and host guest posts.

19. Participate in forum discussions.

20. Create polls, such as: "Which character do you like the most? Why?"

21. Write freelance articles for newspaper and magazines in your target niche market.

22. Sell your books on your website.

23. Play the local writer, and start with small steps: local newspapers and magazines, local radio, sign up for local events.

24. Sell themed swags on your website or Facebook fan page.

25. Set up a launch party.

26. Donate a percentage or a create a limited time revenue for a noble cause.

27. Do a book reading for a group in your community.

28. Donate your books to libraries and community centers.

29. 29Become a HARO source and an influencer on LinkedIn groups.

30. Join a MeetUp group that includes writers and/or readers. If none exist, start one.

31. Write a Book The World Needs

Do you have any book marketing tips you'd like to add to the list? Think outside the box and make your own list.

Think Outside the Box is a marketing cliché yet I have to say that with so many books being published every day, it fits. Do something no one else is doing because this will get you more exposure. Be different. Be first.

Readers may not consciously think about your book the first time they see or hear an ad for it, but subconsciously the information is stored there, somewhere.

The contents of your book may cover subjects similar to other books but your marketing techniques need to be unique. If you think outside the box you can find opportunities for places to display your book. There are always new forms of advertising if you think creatively and use your imagination.

Think about an existing form of media, business cards, or bookmarks. Every author can have them printed without incurring huge costs.

Consider how you print and spread them. If you are just waiting to given them to an agent or a book retailer, this is a terrible waste of time and money. Why don't you talk with your hairstylist or spa salon's manager? I know, it sounds crazy; those places are not normally used to display book ads. Nevertheless, when you leave the salon, you have a business card, a note, a coupon, or a piece of paper for the next appointment. Why can't you print a two-sided business card, one side with the salon contact and the other one with your book? Don't you think this is a win-win deal? If one of the salon's clients wants to recommend your book to a friend, they will pass on the business card and you have the possibility to sell your book to a person you might otherwise never have met.

Something else that you can do is to print some brochures and place them on a table in the salon. People are often bored waiting for their turn so they can read about your book; they have a telephone and they can buy it with a touch on their telephone screen.

I found myself bored in the GP's waiting room. He had a few magazines that were two or three years old—the same magazines I had seen every time. Wouldn't it be nice if there were some brochures with books? Think about this as a cross promotion, especially if your book is about subjects related to medicine such as: books on diets, healthy life style, yoga and meditation. **Think outside the box.**

Now it is your turn. Make a list of a few places you normally would not consider for book advertising. Think why you would not do it and if the answer to this question is nobody else did it then you are a star, you have an idea from **outside the box.**

Six Websites that not many people talk about

1. Listal - www.listal.com

--Join Listal to create lists, share images, get recommendations and much more.

--You can add it to you toolbar and share a post from your blog or a press mention about your book. Listal is a social network based around entertainment including Movies, TV shows, games, DVDs, Music, books, Actors & Actresses, Music artists, Authors and Directors

--List your owned, watched, read or played items and share with friends

--Rate items and add reviews, tags, images, videos & lists

--Organize your Movie/TV, Music, Game or Book collections

--Find similar people

--Rate items and you will automatically find people who share your tastes.

Other features:

Customize your profile.

Create RSS feeds for lists.

Create drag and drop lists annotated with notes and images.

Import and export data.

Track loaned items.

Create flash widgets for your lists and collections.

Private messages.

Discussion forums: View statistics about your collections such as top watched actors or most read authors.

2. Google Books http://books.google.com/googlebooks/partners/index.html

--The Library Project's aim is simple: make it easier for people to find relevant books—

specifically books they wouldn't find any other way, such as those that are out of print, while carefully respecting authors' and publishers' copyrights. Their goal is to work with publishers and libraries to create a comprehensive, searchable, virtual card catalogue of all books in all languages to help users discover new books and publishers discover new readers.

--The best way to get your books included is to speak with your publisher and encourage them to join the Google Books Partner Program. You can direct them to the Partner Program homepage to learn more about how this program can help increase your book sales.

--If you're self-published, or the rights to your book have reverted back to you, you can join the program yourself by sending your books or uploading them in PDF format. Check out Author Resources page to learn more.

Promote Your Books On Google

--Google Books allows publishers and authors to submit their books for inclusion in Google's search results.

Help Users Find Your Books:

--Once you send Google your books (or upload them as PDF files), they will add them to their index for free, by matching the content in your books with user searches. Google Books connects your books with the users who are most interested in buying them.

--Each Google Books result will display the book's title and author, a short excerpt containing the highlighted search terms, and other public data about the book and the author.

3. VDTV Free youtube promotion - VDTV :

Want free promotion for your book trailer? Follow these easy steps:

--You are interested in growing your YouTube channel to gain a bigger audience.

--You send VDTV a link to your favourite video from your own channel, including a small text describing who you are and what you do on your channel.

--Send this information to: VDTV's inbox on YouTube or email them.

--To promote your content the best way possible, add an introduction to the video you send,, explaining what you do on your channel. Provide material that introduces you to your new audience.

--Watch your channel grow!

What are you waiting for? It's 100% free and it will take you two minutes to send the stuff!

Facebook: https://www.facebook.com/Ve...
twitter: http://www.twitter.com/Vend...

Get more exposure for your book trailer!

4. Google+ Communities: https://plus.google.com/communities

--You can expose your books in front of an impressive number of people in just a few minutes. Search a specific genre in communities, join, and share.

Here is an example of what I've done today.

Children's Chapter Books By Bethany Bull

Promotional materials:

A poster

A promotional blog spot

http://authorspromotion.wordpress.com/2014/05/04/childrens-chapter-books-by-bethany-bull/ **and a short video clip**

http://youtu.be/cbqEpoz2MG4

I soon had a list of communities:

Children's Books   1188 members

Parenting   8706 members

The Go-To Parents Community   10651 members

Great Books for Kids   2378 members

Book Club for Kids   259 members

The PLAY Group's Playground   3166 members

Kindle Ebook Promoter   376 members

Reading with Children   693 members

Tools for Raising Smart Kids   405 members

Children's' Books   173 members

Children's Book Reviews, Writers&Illustrators   288 members

Total exposure   28283 people – 15 min work

If only a 10% buy a book that will mean a lot of sales. Good luck Bethany!

5. Mobile Read Forums http://www.mobileread.com/

--Here you have fewer ads, access to post topics, can communicate privately with other members, respond to polls, upload content, submit news about your new release or events and access many other special features.

6. Novelspot Gazette http://gazette.novelspot.net/ and Novelspot Ads http://novelspot.net/_ads offers great opportunities to get exposure at an affordable price.

Part Two

Case study - theory

I will take first a book about teenagers with three subplots: bullying, discrimination, and responsibilities. It can be both, fiction or non-fiction.

Marketing Plan

Overview

Xxxxxxxxxxxxxxx by Xxxxxxx Xxxxxxxxx is a thoughtful piece about one family's values, how to be there for each other, respect, communication, and how these ideas can solve problems in teenagers' and parents' lives.

No family is perfect and life is not perfect. A crisis in a family, or dysfunctional parenting skills, stress, bullying and discrimination can wreak havoc in a person's life forever. When you decide to seek inspiration, look for assistance, or simply read for entertainment, you will find many books, both fiction and non-fiction, on this subject.

Communities can and should do a lot to prevent bullying and discrimination because bullying doesn't happen only between children at school, it can happen everywhere.

The author tells a story of ordinary people who leave a positive imprint on their community by making a simple choice; the characters choose to react with selflessness, with gentleness rather than violence, with love and kindness rather than hate or anger. Any of us can choose to be a kind and empathic person, to help make a difference in someone else's life, at home, in the communities where we live, or over the Internet.

Xxxxxxxxxxxxxxxxxxx by Xxxxxx Xxxxxxxxx will inspire the readers to talk and think about feelings, responsibilities, and choices.

About the author:

Xxxxxxxx Xxxxxxxxxx is the author of other several books, (list them). He is a contributor to **Parenting Today Magazine** and a counselor dealing with parenting and teens issues. Xxxxxx Xxxxxxx is an educational psychologist, former teacher, and active social worker for supporting teens.

The author has led many seminars and workshops on subjects such as: victims of bullying, parenting solutions, relational aggression, racism, and discrimination.

For his latest non-fiction book, xxxxxxxxx xxxxxxxxxxxxx xxxxxxxxxxx, he won (name the prize) and has made appearances in TV shows, Writers Conferences and Radio Interviews.

To find out more about the author visit his website at . . . Here you will find all his social media links or see his online media press kit at . . .

Market Analysis - SWOT

Strengths – All three subplots are daily on the media outlets agenda

- o The author's experience shows that the book is written by someone who knows well this subject.

- o The marketing niche is large: parents, social workers, organizations and associations who fight bullying, racism and discrimination, and support groups for teens or parents, teachers;

- o The book covers important and useful information.

Weaknesses – It will be out on the market when summer holiday begins, so there is not a possibility for presentation in school libraries.

Opportunities – The book will be released just in time to be presented at Book Expo America and Chicago Tribune's Printer's Row Fest. It has also been put on the list for the Library of Congress National Book Festival, Miami Book Fair International, London Briefcase 2014, and Summer Exhibition of the Royal Academy.

Threats – By its subject, it may limit the target audience a bit, addressing more to people who are aware of this social issues than to regular readers

Marketing – Target Market and Positioning - People expected to buy this book are: independent booksellers, middle grade school libraries, parents, communities and support groups, social workers, counselors, teachers and other professionals involved in social issues, organization, and foundations.

Promotion

Cover reveal tour 1st June-7th June

Hosts for cover reveal and a short synopsis announcing the release date

I Am A Reader (Int)

Read Now Sleep Later (Int)

Kate @ Ex Libris (INT)

Mother Daughter Book Reviews (INT)

Wall-to-wall books (US)

Ellie @ Spiced Latte Reads (US)

Live To Read ~Krystal (USA/CAN)

Tressa's Wishful Endings (US)

Batch of Books (US)

Auggie-Talk (US)

Mary Had a Little Book Blog (US)

Diane Estrella @ That's What I'm Here For. . . (US)

Alicia @ Addicted Readers (INT)

Simple Wyrdings (US)

Icefairy's Treasure Chest (Int)

A Belle's Tales (INT)

By The Book (US)

Books à la Mode (INT)

Bookworm Lisa (Int)

Gator Mommy Reviews (US)

Savings in Seconds (US)

Chapter by Chapter (Int)

Step Into Fiction (INT)

Ketch's Book Nook (INT)

Author Jesse Kimmel-Freeman (INT)

The Windy Pages (US)

Author Anna Kyss (US)

Living As We (CAN)

Susan Heim on Writing (US)

We made promotional materials and swags that will be distributed to summer camps, schools, and supplied to foundations and interested associations.

We set up an anti-bullying campaign for two weeks, just before the end of school, with speaking engagements at the city hall and a few high schools' libraries.

We arranged three book signing events with the major booksellers in town.

We set up a radio interview at LA Talk Radio, with host Allen Cardoza. The show "Answers 4 the Family," is booked for late August.

We arranged for a Give Away campaign on GoodReads in July.

We set up a free kindle promotion on Amazon in the first 25 days after publication date.

An ARC was sent to Family Tree Magazine, Midwest Book Review, and Kirkus Reviews.

A blog tour From 1st July-15th July, was organized by Authors PR Madi Preda. Reviews and contained interviews from the blog tour.

Tour Hosts

http://2kidsandtiredbooks.blogspot.com/
http://books-camilleelise4.blogspot.com/
http://abookbloggersdiary.blogspot.com/
http://dixie-afewofmyfavoritethings.blogspot.com/
http://www.amamascorneroftheworld.com/
http://www.amamasrant.com/
http://booksbyamotherstouch.blogspot.com/
http://anovelsource.blogspot.com/
http://aseaofbooks.blogspot.com/
http://alvincromer4trr.blogspot.com/
http://ascendingbutterfly.blogspot.com/
http://auggie-talk.blogspot.com/
http://www.authorexposure.com/
http://autumnbluesreviews.com/
http://wendisbookcorner.blogspot.com/
http://www.whatyoureadingnow.blogspot.com/
http://www.winterwrite.com/
http://shumphreys.blogspot.com/
http://kittycrochettwo.blogspot.com/
http://www.thejoyofbooking.com/
http://www.fsbmedia.com/www.jsknowlton.blogspot.com

http://blog.theloudlibrarian.net/
http://thepaperbackpursuer.blogspot.com/
http://www.fsbmedia.com/www.thethingsweread.blogspot.com
http://www.theuniquereviewer.com/
http://books.tinaarnoldi.com/
http://totallybookedsolid.blogspot.com/
http://tryingtogogreen.blogspot.com/
http://soapboxinmymind.blogspot.com/
http://spooklights.blogspot.com/
http://startfromscratchblog.blogspot.it/
http://www.fsbmedia.com/www.takingyourstand.blogspot.com
http://tgteecher.blogspot.com/
http://www.dianeestrella.com/
http://www.fsbmedia.com/www.thebookaddict.net
http://www.thebookwormblog.com/

*Note: I am using different hosts for cover reveal than for the release. This way the book gains more exposure and some of the participants in the cover reveal might participate on the release blog tour as well.

Press releases sent to the following placements:

Google News - Z100 FM New York

The View - Wall Street Journal

Cosmopolitan - The O'Reilly Factor

Women's World - Fox News

Dateline NBC - Los Angeles Times

The Insider - Self Magazine

Us Magazine - KABC Los Angeles

Star Magazine - Redbook

People Magazine - Book TV

KNBC Los Angeles - Seventeen

ESPN - In Touch Magazine

KFI Los Angeles - Allure

WABC New York - Access Hollywood

KLAC Los Angeles - Extra

USA Today - E-Entertainment TV

CBS Early Show - KIIS-FM Los Angeles

Your World (Cavuto) - Maxim Magazine

MTV News - Good Morning America

Target Agents – social issues:

www.miriamaltshulerliteraryagency.com

www.literaryrejections.com

www.irenegoodman.com

http://awfulagent.com/agents/eddie-schneider

www.jdlit.com

www.lowensteinassociates.com

www.jonathanpegg.com

http://doncongdon.com/agents.shtml

http://www.publishersmarketplace.com

www.agentquery.com

Query letters were sent in accordance with their guideline submission, based on the

marketing plan from above.

Target Publishers – humanities and social issues:

US and Canada

Para Publishing

Barricade Books

Christian Education Publishers

Cleiss Press

Cowley Publications/Rowman & Littlefield

Lexington Books/Rowman & Littlefield

Scarecrow Press/Rowman & Littlefield

Farrar, Straus and Giroux

UK

Archon Books

Black Rose Books

Blackwell Publishers UK+US

Octopus Publishing Group

Perseus – parenting

Query letters were sent directly to publishers, in accordance with their guideline submission, based on the marketing plan from above.

Authors PR Review for the book – I give it five out of five stars

This is a book for a lifetime. It is an essential story for readers wanting to understand bullying and discrimination within communities—perfect for teens, parents, grandparents, and educators alike.

The teenage years are filled with growth, promise, and trials. During this time teenagers are faced with life-changing decisions and challenges. Often these dilemmas are not easy to answer or resolve.

In this book, Xxxxxxxxx Xxxxxxxxxxxx, a prominent counselor, educational psychologist, former teacher, and active social worker explores issues of bullying and discrimination, and guides readers to a better understanding of themselves, their strengths, desires, and their role in community.

The story offers help for teenagers and at-risk groups to integrate into their community so they may realize their visions. In an entertaining style, the author bridges the gap between education and life, and inspires teenagers to find ways to boost their self-esteem, avoid peer pressure, and handle the daily stresses of being different or bullied because of religion, race, or cultural norms.

As a continuous militant for equal rights, fighting against discrimination, the author promotes youth leadership and high moral principles. Xxxxxxxxx Xxxxxxx knows how to talk to teenagers and how to help them prepare for adulthood. Its hands-on approach and personal style make this engaging book a must-have for teens as well as for parents, grandparents, people who choose to stand on their side, as well as anyone else who has the opportunity to influence young people.

Note: If the book is fiction you introduce a paragraph by saying ,"Although this is a work of fiction, the subject is of great importance in today's world."

Case Study – Publicity Campaign for *Changing Spaces* by Nancy King

"What would you do if you woke up in your usual life, and by the end of the day, everything had changed?"

This is the question Nancy King poses in her newest book, *Changing Spaces,* as she introduces us to Laura Feldman, who suddenly loses the "life" she has lived as a married woman.

When her husband of forty years suddenly wants a divorce, shaken-to-her-core, Laura Feldman embarks on a bumpy ride from her black & white Midwestern life to the bold colors of New Mexico. In this new landscape where anything might happen–and does–Laura finds inspiration, strength, and transformation in the friendship of three Santa Fe women who help her walk the winding road to self-discovery and the home of her heart.

"Location. Location. Location. Nancy King gets it right when she explores how a woman radically changes her life by changing her location.
—Judith Fein, author of *Life Is a Trip: The Transformative Magic of Travel*"

"Heartbreak turns to intrigue. A season of grief leads to a wig, a closet, a script, cookie recipes, new friendships, and a wide-open future."

   —JEANNE MURRAY WALKER, Author of *Geography of Memory*

Changing Spaces grew out of a conversation Nancy King had with a woman who said:

"That was before I lost my life."

Nancy King's novel *The Stones Speak* was optioned for a film, and won first place in the New Mexico Presswomen Communications Contest. A prolific playwright and essayist, King has also written seven nonfiction books—most recently *Dancing With Wonder: Self-Discovery Through Stories*—an exploration of her storymaking, writing and drama workshops in the US and abroad.

She feels fortunate to be privy to the stories people share.

Nancy King lives in Santa Fe, New Mexico where she works as an educational consultant, weaves, writes, and finds inspiration hiking in the mountains. She is a contributing writer to the online journal: yourlifeisatrip.com. Her writing can be found at www.yourlifeisatrip.com/home/author/nancyking.

Please visit Nancy King's website at http://www.nancykingstories.com to read excerpts of her books and find information about her various workshops.

Reading Guide on LitLovers

Radio Interview:
Santa Fe Radio Cafe (KSFR)
6.February.2014
http://www.santaferadiocafe.org/podcasts/?p=5565

Radio Interview:
Majority Report/Women's Voices (KZYX)
20.January.2014
http://www.kzyx.org/index.php/talk-shows/politics-and-public-affairs/womens-voices/
entry/archive-womens-voices-january-27-2013

Authors PR Review – five stars out of five:

Life is a journey and you have to go on

Changing Spaces is a gripping tale of one woman's self-discovery after she lost her 'life'-an unexpected divorce after 40 years of marriage. Powerfully felt and beautiful written, full of wonder and heart-wrenching sorrow, *Changing Spaces* by Nancy King is a novel that focuses on the bittersweet process of reinventing a new life for Laura, a 60 year-old woman whose marriage was the center of her life.

Zach and Laura's story unfolds in a pattern of domination by a husband determined to assert his mastery over his wife and a wife dedicated to her husband's well being. Her life as she has known it for forty years ends suddenly when her husband Zach decides to end their marriage because of his love for a younger woman.

Shocked, Laura runs from her husband and her past, into an airport shuttle that happens to be going to Santa Fe, where she meets three women whose friendship help her face her loss of self-confidence, heartbreak, and despair. She discovers ways to reconnect with her lost self as well as create a new and meaningful life. By finding the wherewithal to make difficult choices, Laura transforms herself in surprising ways.

Will Zach and Laura resolve their marital crisis? If so, how? You will find the answers by reading *Changing Spaces*, a stunning book to be savored in a quiet, reflective mood.

Marketing Plan for *Changing Spaces* by Nancy King

Overview

Changing Spaces is a book that inspires readers to think about what it means to have a healthy and impactful life, whether you are in a relationship or not, and offers insights on marriage, relationships, and the single life.

SWOT Analysis

- The book transmits a powerful and inspirational message about what it means to lose and find one's self.

- *Changing Spaces* has mass market potential. Many readers are interested in books about self-improvement and relationship in fiction and non- fiction.

- The target market is easy to identify.

Opportunities

--*Changing Spaces* may attract a large category of readers, women of all ages, cultures, and locations

--Nancy King's book is published in electronic and paperback editions so it could be promoted with booksellers, in libraries, and in gift shops.

--It is holiday season and a promotion campaign in holiday resorts sounds just right to me (flyers distributed in hotels, campsites, travel agencies).

-- The author has published many books of fiction and nonfiction so promoting *Changing Spaces* may generate more exposure and increase sales for the other books as well.

Threats

For Changing Spaces, the audience is very well defined but in the same time restrained to a certain audience.

Positioning

People expected to buy Nancy's books are women from different cultures, demographic areas, and ages. We are focused on women who are interested in self-improvement, relationships, self-esteem, as well as women who have to recreate their life after a divorce, or face major challenges in their lives and need to learn how to reinvent themselves.

Promotion

- Create promotional materials such as flyers, brochures, and business cards for *Changing Spaces*, which is our case study, with a mention about the other books.

- Identify communities, support groups, and organizations that support single women.

- Promote with Google + Communities.

- Facebook Groups for women short teasers.

- Twitter using customized hashtags.

- Magazines focused on lifestyle, women, and relationships.

- Interviews with independent radio stations focused on the same topics.

- Contact libraries. They may sponsor readers' groups.

- Posters, if the author will print them, to be used for her speaking engagements, together with other promotional materials.

- Identify coaches on NLP for storytelling and references.

- A major objective is to offer a few copies for reviews.

- If the author agrees we will organize a virtual book tour.

- Blog posts on AUTHORS PROMOTION and on Book blogs

- Madi Preda Authors PR will have an interview with the author to be posted across social media.

- As a contributor to Angie's Diary Magazine and LitArt Magazine – Liphar, Authors PR Madi Preda will submit a review and the interview for publication.

- Last but not least, there is a need for the author's website to be submitted to search engines and build back links.

Now we will follow the marketing plan.

Promotional Material

An electronic newsletter has been created with SMORE and you can check it out here:

https://www.smore.com/h4a1s

Up to now it has been sent to 96 booksellers

--39 in US

--21 in Canada

--5 to American Bookshops in Holland

--21 to (a new idea) gift shops and libraries on cruises lines

We have already had replies from Orion Cruises, Captains Club-Celebrity Cruises,and Crown and Anchor.

Blog Post for AUTHORS PROMOTION

Check it here http://authorspromotion.wordpress.com/2014/05/22/changing-spaces-by-nancy-king-2/

This post was sent to Huffington post – Life After Divorce – The Internet Newspaper and Psychology Today – New York, requiring an interview or an article.

Another promotional spot on book blogs

"Changing Spaces is a book that inspires readers to build meaningful lives, whether or not they are in a relationship. It helps readers to answer two questions: Who are they? What are they living? The novel offers powerful insights on relationships and life as a single person. I recommend *Changing Spaces* to anyone who is suffering after a divorce. There are lots of thoughts about healing as we follow Laura Feldman's journey."

This will be used together with the review and author's biography or with the interview.

Teasers to use for posting adds:

--What are the choices you can start to make after divorce? Read *Changing Spaces* by Nancy King to find some answers.

--What can you do when a relationship you entered with hope is dissolved? Discover how one woman remakes her life in the novel, *Changing Spaces* by Nancy King.

--Follow Laura Feldman in *Changing Spaces* by Nancy King as she moves beyond pain and finds her lost self. Life goes on. There can be transformation after divorce.

--Thrive after divorce by reading *Changing Spaces* by Nancy King. It gives you ideas on how to reinvent your life.

--*Changing Spaces* by Nancy King explores how it is possible to empower ourselves to change and work through the grief after divorce.

--Divorce is a major challenge and Nancy King, in her novel, *Changing Spaces*, offers healing encouragement.

--All single women should read Nancy King's book, *Changing Spaces.*

--Single Ladies! Here is *Changing Spaces* by Nancy King. Make a new and whole life from one that is broken.

--Go get what you deserve even if it's hard to find. *Changing Spaces* by Nancy King.

--In the emptiness after divorce, the beauty of life comes into focus. *Changing Spaces* by Nancy King

--*Changing Spaces* by Nancy King. An empty page leaves room for new words to fill it.

--Crumbled dreams make it possible to dig a deeper foundation for new dreams. Nancy King tells about this in *Changing Spaces.*

--Down to nothing means anything is possible. Read *Changing Spaces* to see how true this is.

--Happiness could be waiting around the corner. *Changing Spaces* by Nancy King is waiting for you.

--Be real with yourself even when it hurts. *Changing Spaces* by Nancy King.

--Nancy King, in *Changing Spaces* shows you that you can start over at anytime. Hit the reset button and move on.

Magazines to submit articles

Happy Woman Magazine	- sent
Marie Claire Magazine	- sent
Being Single Magazine	- sent
The Believer	-sent
Eye on Life Magazine	- sent
Whidbey Life Magazine	- sent
Apple Magazine	- sent
Huffington post – Life After Divorce – The Internet Newspaper	- sent
Psychology Today – New York	- sent

Website Optimization – done

Backlinks – a few examples from 65

http://bm8.com.cn/Alexa/Index.asp?domain=www.nancykingstories.com

http://blogsearch.google.com/blogsearch?hl=zh-CN&ie=UTF-8&q=www.nancykingstories.com&lr=

http://blogsearch.google.cn/blogsearch?q=www.nancykingstories.com&sa=N&tab=vb

http://blog.hexun.com/group/commontag.aspx?searchTag=www.nancykingstories.com

http://baidu68.com.cn/tool.asp?weburl=www.nancykingstories.com

http://alexa.win2000.net/Index.asp?url=www.nancykingstories.com

http://alexa.win2000.net/?url=www.nancykingstories.com

http://alexa.3m2n.com/alexa/?url=www.nancykingstories.com

Website was submitted to 70 search engines including Google, Bing, AOL, WebCrawler, EntireWeb, and many others.

Nancy King, interviewed by Madi Preda from Authors PR

Nancy King is the author of seven books of nonfiction, four novels, and many plays and essays. She is currently works as a consultant focusing on the development of innovative literacy and drama programs in schools, teaches writing, and works with older women, helping them to find ways to re-invent their lives. One of her novels, *The Stones Speak*, was selected as a finalist in the New Mexico Books Award – 2009, was optioned for a film, and won the award for best novel by the New Mexico Presswomen's Association.

Hello Nancy and thank you for taking time to answer my questions. Where does your passion for stories, questions about identity, and the importance of self-discovery come from? I ask because it seems that all that your books explore these themes.

Stories saved my life. When I was a child, growing up in a difficult family, I would hide in a safe place, close my eyes, imagine a theatre in my head, and tell myself a story about a heroic girl with all the qualities I didn't think I had. Afterward I always felt better. As an adult, dealing with a catastrophic illness and challenging life situations, telling myself stories gave me the energy to face and confront what I needed to do. In my novels, as well as in life, the stories we are told about ourselves, the stories we tell ourselves, as well as the stories we tell others, play a large part in the development of who we are.

Self-discovery and identity are intertwined. I grew up, metaphorically speaking, in a "fun house mirror." My sense of self grew out of, and was dependent upon what others told me about myself. Much of what they said turned out to be distorted, damaging, and not true. It took many years before I began to realize that the stories told about me were lies, told to cover up what really happened, to protect those who had hurt me. Even after I began to suss out enough of the truth to understand why I had made so many bad choices, changing my view of myself was complicated and problematic. So much of how I had lived my life was based on what I had been told and, as a result, what I experienced. Although these old voices still live inside me they no longer have the power they once did and I am freer to live as I choose.

You have written so many books that there is not enough room to talk about all of them. We should have an interview for each of them sometime. Please tell us now

about your latest one, *Changing Spaces* and the main character, Laura Feldman. What inspired you to write this story?

A few years ago I was invited to a Christmas party where I admired the hostess's unusual crèche. In response she shrugged and said, "I made it before I lost my life." I didn't know her well enough to ask the myriad questions that came to mind, but it turned out that her husband of 40 years had come home one night, told her he was in love with another woman and wanted a divorce. This was bad enough, but she was a corporate wife and he asked her to resign from all the boards she was now on so his new wife could be on them. Within the next three weeks I heard stories from two women whose husbands had left them for younger women, as well as reading an article in the New York Times by a woman who had once extolled the joys of being a stay-at-home wife and mother, but was now writing about being dumped by her husband of 40 years who wanted to marry a younger woman.

I couldn't get the words, "That was before I lost my life," out of my mind. I kept wondering what it might be like to suddenly lose the only life you had known for 40 years. How does one make a new life after 60? As a result, I created the character of Laura and the novel *Changing Spaces* was born.

Why write about divorce? Why have Laura flee to Santa Fe? You describe Santa Fe as a place where people seem to have an unusual sense of communication, where it is possible to create one's own way of living and being. Is Santa Fe a special place?

Divorce ends life as we know it even if a couple has children. I've been divorced twice and each time I had to make fundamental choices about who I was and who I wanted to be. I was forced to decide how I wanted to live given that the life I had known was finished. Although my situations differed from Laura's, the question of what one does after divorce intrigued me. I situated the novel in Santa Fe because I find it to be an extraordinary place. Perhaps it's the confluence of cultures, the mountains, the geographical isolation . . . I don't really know. I came to Santa Fe without planning or intention and discovered the power of being known without anyone knowing my history. No one reminded me about something I'd said or done years ago. My soul and spirit flew free. I could be who I was instead of the person people thought I was or needed me to be.

Why did you choose a woman as your main character? Do you think that it is easier for men to recover after divorce or is it just as painful for them as for women?

I think it's impossible to generalize. People without financial means tend to have fewer choices and none of them might be good. The one who leaves often has an easier time than the one who is left. I chose a woman as my main character because many women in my generation were told that our job was to take care of our husbands, to put them first. I was "lucky" in a way because no man ever supported me financially or emotionally. I've always had to work, and for years I was a single mother with no child support. I needed to earn money but I chose to focus on creating a career for myself rather than simply looking for a job. This was much easier to do then than it is now because then there were fewer gatekeepers and bean counters. Experience mattered as much as educational degrees. In fact, I got my PhD ten years after I'd been promoted to full professor. That's unlikely to happen these days.

How many 'Laura Feldmans' do you know in real life? How easy is it for people to move on and make a new life after a life-changing event?

Laura Feldman, like many women of her age, was taught to put her husband's happiness and well being above and before her own. When the marriage ended, a vacuum was created, requiring her to make new choices. I don't think it is ever easy to move on, to make a truly new life. There are people who remarry, thinking they've chosen someone different, only to realize the new spouse is a version of their previous one. Actually changing one's life is challenging and yet, in my experience, having the wherewithal to face unpleasant truths, bewildering feelings, puzzling memories, and difficult situations, has made it possible for me to say, "This is the best time of my life."

What themes are important to you to share with your readers in *Changing Spaces*?

I write from what I describe as a theatre in my head. The characters I create take on lives of their own, and although they are crafted by me, through my experience, they aren't me. Since I think no one can tell anyone else what a story means without killing the story, I prefer not to tell readers what themes are important to me because I think what really matters is what readers think and feel, the themes and ideas that are significant to them.

I think human potential is endless and I want to ask you something. How far should we dream and how high should we set our goals in life in order not to be disillusioned?

Dreams and goals are about possibility, about knowing where your interests and passions lie. When I was in my twenties I wanted to teach using all the arts and was constantly told this was impossible, that I had to focus on one and become expert in that area, something I was unable to make myself do. Then, many years later, when I found a way to teach world literature in the University of Delaware Honors Program, I incorporated art, music, drama, movement, and stories into my teaching, thus fulfilling the dream I'd had when I was so much younger. Although I never gave up, I also never thought I'd find a way to do this given the rigid structure of university departments. And yet, without conscious action, this desire influenced every choice I made, leading to the moment when I had the opportunity to teach in ways that were important to my students and me.

Please, can you tell me more about your literacy programs?

To me, literacy is about being able to read, write, and speak with authenticity, fluency, and confidence. Given that I often work with people who have difficulty reading, writing and speaking, I use a multi-faceted approach that builds upon the skills people already have—telling stories. I recently worked with 8th grade middle-school students, helping them to write a memoir of an important event in their lives. Almost all of them had failed standardized literacy tests, most students had never written more than a paragraph, and for many, English was their second language.

I usually begin teaching by telling a traditional story, which acts as a container for the session to follow. Then, as a way of connecting verbal and nonverbal knowing, students paint and/or sculpt an image from an abstract prompt (paint an image of courage or sculpt an image of possibility) in less than a minute. More time results in increased anguish. After the imagemaking, participants write words that come to mind, thus anchoring the image in their consciousness.

What follows, depends upon the focus of the group. In the case of the 8th graders, the imagemaking helped to evoke important aspects of their stories and eased their anxiety about writing. Much to their surprise, but not mine, they wrote powerful and moving memoirs which they then shared with their classmates and visitors who came to a celebration of the book that had been made from their stories.

An exploration of my work with stories, both in the US and abroad, can be found in *Dancing With Wonder: Self-Discovery Through Stories*. You can read an excerpt of it on my website:

And finally, what are you working on right now? Can you tell us a few words about your work in progress?

I'm working on a novel, currently titled, *Opening Gates*. It's based on experiences I had years ago, when I was nineteen, hired to be a summer recreational therapist in charge of a building of women in a large mental hospital. The young protagonist, Rennie, is thrust into a world where missteps have terrifying consequences. As she learns to negotiate the rollercoaster world of the hospital, she develops the courage to act in ways she could never have imagined before taking the job.

Thank you for being with us. I hope that all the visitors on my blog will enjoy your interview and I hope to have you back with us soon. It was a pleasure to talk with you today and judging by the responses to the post about your books, I think my readers are curious to hear author Nancy King's thoughts. I wish you good luck and many readers.

You can read more about Nancy King's book, Changing Spaces here

Note: I have to stop now with my case study because it is time for my book to be polished by an editor and prepared for publishing. I hope that you will find a few useful ideas in it and I look forward to hearing what you think about *How To Promote and Market Your Book.*

If you read this message that means you bought the book and for that I am grateful.

You can always contact me at authorspr@gmail.com and we can discuss anytime about the problems encountered with your book's promotion.

Thank you and I am waiting to hear about your successes.

Resources

Where to Send Press Release Sites

www.newsvine.com

www.prlog.org

www.pitchengine.com

www.i-newsvire.com

www.openpr.com

www.newswiretoday.com

www.free-press-release.com

www.myprgenie.com

www.beforeitsnews.com

www.prfire.co.uk

www.prbuzz.com

www.onlineprnews.com

www.pressbox.co.uk

www.BriefingWire.com

Editors

Cynthia Baumann: Based in PA, Cynthia edits mostly fiction, and enjoys science fiction and fantasy, including urban fantasy and supernatural genres, and historical fiction.

Virginia Bowen: Virginia provides all levels of editing for non-fiction, fiction, children's, and marketing publications.

JoAnne Dyer: Seattle based, nonfiction, web content, and mysteries.

Melinda Fulton: Specializes in editing romance (content, copyediting, proofreading)

Kendall Margaret Hoover: Edits everything from blogs to business materials, resumes to cover letters, book proposals to books.

Michelle Hutchinson, she edits and proofreads manuscripts across a variety of fiction and non-fiction genres.

Caroline Kaiser: Toronto-based, Caroline's list includes YA, sci-fi, memoir and historical fiction.

Alice Peck: edits and coaches authors at every stage of the process—concept, book proposal, first draft, or publisher's revisions. Her interests include: memoir/autobiography, narrative, spirituality and religion, social issues, literary and popular fiction

Laurie Price: Writer, Copy Editor/Proofreader, works on business books, novels, children's books and bilingual textbooks, as well as freelance editing and proofreading.

Word Works: Charleston, SC based Mary B. Johnston specializes in non-fiction work.

List of Book Bloggers – General Fiction

Sky Ink
http://skyink.net

Slayra
http://pinkgum.blogspot.com/

Smutty Dirty Bitch
http://smuttydirtybitch.blogspot.com/

Socrates' Book Review Blog
http://socratesbookreviews.blogspot.com/

So Many Books, So Little Time
http://smbslt.blogspot.com

So Many Books, So Little Time
http://somanybookssolittletimeblog.blogspot.com/

Starcrossed
http://starcrossedreviews.blogspot.com

Sunshine's Book Review's
http://mycrazythoughtprocess.blogspot.com/

Surrounded by Books Reviews
http://surroundedbybooksreviews.blogspot.com

Surrounded By Words
http://surroundedbywords.blogspot.com

Sweeping Me
http://www.sweepingme.com

A Tale of Many Reviews
http://ataleofmanyreviews.blogspot.com/

Tales Between the Pages
http://talesbetweenthepages.com

Tales of Time
http://www.talesoftime1.blogspot.com/

Tales of Whimsy…
http://www.talesofwhimsy.com

Talk About Authors
http://talkaboutauthors.blogspot.com

Tammy's Book Reviews
http://tammysbookreviews.blogspot.com/

TC-Booked Up
www.tc-bookedup.blogspot.com

Teresa's Reading Corner
http://www.teresasreadingcorner.com

These Pretty Words
http://theseprettywords.com

Thoughts in Progress
http://www.masoncanyon.blogspot.com

Tigris Eden's Garden of Books
www.tigriseden.blogspot.com

Tinas Book Reviews
http://www.tinasbookreviews.com

Today I'm Reading
http://www.todayimreading.blogspot.com/

The Traveling Reader
http://thetravelingreader.wordpress.com

TREASURED SPOT BOOK REVIEWS
http://treasuredspotbookreviews.com

Trees and Ink
http://treesandink.wordpress.com

The True Book Addict
http://thetruebookaddict.blogspot.com/

Turning the Pages
http://bookbybookreview.blogspot.com/

Twilight and Other Dreams
http://twilightandotherdreams.blogspot.com/

Two Readers Reviews
www.tworeadersreviews.blogspot.com

Vanessa Linna
http://vanessalinna.blogspot.com

Warrior's Heart Novels
http://warriorsheartnovels.com

The Weekly Kat Scan
http://theweeklykatscan.blogspot.com/

The Well Read Voyageur
http://wellreadvoyageur.blogspot.com/

What Book to Read
www.whatbooktoread.com

What Red Read
http://whatredread.blogspot.com/

What's On the Bookshelf
http://whatsonthebookshelf-jen.blogspot.com

What You Read
http://petekarnas.wordpress.com

Wicked Without Knowing It
http://wickedwithoutknowingit.wordpress.com/

witchever
http://www.crossroadreviews.com

Without a Book
http://withoutabook.wordpress.com/

The Wonky Bookcase
http://wonkybookcase.blogspot.com/

The Word Fiend
http://thewordfiend.blogspot.com

WordNerdBird
http://wordnerdbird.blogspot.com

Words I Write Crazy
http://writingcrazyme.blogspot.com/

Words of Wisdom from The Scarf Princess
http://wowfromthescarfprincess.blogspot.com/

Workaday Reads
http://www.workadayreads.com

Wordsmith Pages
http://wordsmithpages.com/wordpress/

World of Book Reviews
http://worldofbookreviews.blogspot.com

The Wormhole
http://wormyhole.blogspot.com

Worn Pages and Dusty Shelves
http://wornpagesanddustyshelves.wordpress.com/

Your Shelf Life
http://yourshelflife.com

Zephyrus Archives
http://www.zephyrusarchives.com

Zodiac Book Reviews
http://zodiacbookreviews.blogspot.com/

2 Kids and Tired Books
http://2kidsandtiredbooks.blogspot.com

5 Line Reviews
http://fivelines5.blogspot.com/

Novel Niche: A Place for Books
http://www.novelniche.wordpress.com

A Novel Review
http://anovelreview.blogspot.com/

OEBooks
http://oebooks.blogspot.com

Okbolover
http://okbolover.wordpress.com

On a Book Bender: Tales of an Unapologetic Addict
http://onabookbender.wordpress.com

Once Upon a Prologue
http://www.faithunfurled.blogspot.com

One Book Per Week
http://onebookperweek.ca

List of Book Bloggers –adventure, mystery, thrillers

Addicted to Books
http://imaddicted2yabooks.blogspot.com/

Ashley Suzanne
http://www.ashley–suzanne.blogspot.com/

The Book Bash Reviews
http://thebookbashreviews.blogspot.com/

The Book Bell
http://thebookbell.blogspot.com

Book Bite Reviews
http://bookbitereviews.blogspot.com/

Caught in the Pages
http://www.caughtinthepages.blogspot.com/

IReadUpAStorm
http://ireadupastorm.blogspot.com/

My Little Book Blog
http://meganslittlebookblog.blogspot.com/

Novel Goddess
http://www.novelgoddess.com/

Outhouse Reviews
www.inthe-outhouse.blogspot.com

Princess Pandoryss
http://princesspandoryss.blogspot.com/

Reading Hobby
http://readinghobby2.blogspot.com

Secrets of a Bookie
http://secretsofabookie.blogspot.com/

Spine Chills
http://spinechills.blogspot.com

Waking At Dawn
http://wakingatdawn.blogspot.com/

We Fancy Books
http://wefancybooks.blogspot.com/

Sites to Promote free and discounted book

http://ereadernewstoday.com/

http://www.pixelofink.com/

http://www.peoplereads.com/

http://www.thefussylibrarian.com/for-authors/

http://www.fkbooksandtips.com/for-authors/free-kindle-book-submission-form/

http://home.bookbub.com/home/

http://www.indiesunlimited.com/freebie-friday/

http://freebooksy.com/

http://kindlenationdaily.com/

http://www.worldliterarycafe.com/content/find-your-books-wings

http://bargainbooksy.com/sell-more-books/

http://kindlemojo.com/

http://www.thekindlebookreview.net/advertise-here/

http://www.totallyfreestuff.com/

http://www.icravefreebies.com/contact/

http://fireapps.blogspot.ca/p/app-developers-authors.html

http://bargainebookhunter.com/feature-your-book/

http://www.freebookdude.com/p/list-your-free-book.html

http://blog.booksontheknob.org/about-this-blog-and-contact-info

http://freebooksy.com/editorial-submissions

http://www.thatbookplace.com/free-promo-submissions/

http://addictedtoebooks.com/submission

http://bookgorilla.com/

http://www.kindleboards.com/free-book-promo/

http://indiebookoftheday.com/authors/free-on-kindle-listing/

http://www.ebooklister.net/submit.php

http://kindlebookpromos.luckycinda.com/?page_id=283

http://thedigitalinkspot.blogspot.com.es/p/contact-us.html

http://freekindlefiction.blogspot.co.uk/p/tell-us-about-free-books.html

http://www.freeebooksdaily.com/

http://www.freebookshub.com/authors/

http://www.frugal-freebies.com/

http://www.ereaderiq.com/about/

http://askdavid.com/free-book-promotion

http://ebookshabit.com/about-us/

http://www.ereaderperks.com/about/

http://snickslist.com/books/place-ad/

http://freekindlefiction.blogspot.ca/p/featured-post.html

http://awesomegang.com/submit-your-book/

http://thefrugalereader.wufoo.com/forms/frugal-freebie-submissions/

http://www.goodkindles.net/p/why-should-i-submit-my-book-here.html

http://www.blackcaviar-bookclub.com/free-book-promotion.html#.UXFB27XYeOc

http://digitalbooktoday.com/12-top-100-submit-your-free-book-to-be-included-on-this-list/

http://www.kornerkonnection.com/index.html?fb=ebookkornerkafe

http://www.dailycheapreads.com/

http://www.freeebooksdaily.com/p/contact.html

http://bookgoodies.com/submit-your-free-kindle-days/highlight-your-free-kindle-days/

http://indiebookoftheday.com

http://pixelscroll.com/feature-your-product-2/

http://www.ebookbargainsuk.com/price.html

UK

http://uk.hundredzeros.com/

http://freekindlefiction.blogspot.co.uk/

http://flurriesofwords.blogspot.co.uk/

http://ebookdealoftheday.co.uk/submissions/

http://www.dailycheapreads.co.uk/

http://www.indie-book-bargains.co.uk

http://www.xtme.de/submitting-a-free-e-book-to-xtmeenglishbooks/ (German site for English books)

Facebook Groups and Pages to Promote Your Book

https://www.facebook.com/onlyromance

https://www.facebook.com/ebooksfreefreefree

https://www.facebook.com/pages/Short-Stories-Flash-Fiction-Stories/692915047420207

https://www.facebook.com/pages/UK-Kindle-Book-Lovers/175617412524192

https://www.facebook.com/kindle

https://www.facebook.com/pages/The-Frugal-eReader/101086513289732

https://www.facebook.com/BookJunkiesLibrary

https://www.facebook.com/IndieKindleWLC

https://www.facebook.com/weloveebooks

https://www.facebook.com/Bargain.eBook.Hunter

https://www.facebook.com/TheKindleObsessed

https://www.facebook.com/KindleNation

https://www.facebook.com/ebookimpresario

https://www.facebook.com/earthsbooknook

https://www.facebook.com/AontheC

https://www.facebook.com/freeebookdeal?sk=wall

https://www.facebook.com/iauthor?sk=wall

https://www.facebook.com/kuforum

https://www.facebook.com/pages/Kindle-Finds/217115528350246

https://www.facebook.com/IndieBookLounge

https://www.facebook.com/groups/kindlefreebooks/

News Portals

Advertising & Marketing News (*)

American Public Media: Marketplace

Arizona Central (AZ)

BioSpace®

Boston Globe (MA)

CaliforniaNewswire® (*)

CEO World

Cincinnati Enquirer (OH)

DailyHerald (IL)

DealBreaker

eNewsChannels (**)

eZanga

FloridaNewswire (*)

Free Beer & Hot Wings Radio Show

Investing Daily

MassachusettsNewswire (*)

NewsOK (OK)

News Channel 9 - ABC (NY)

News on 6 - KOTV (OK)

Minyanville

PressEnterprise (CA)

Publishers Newswire (**)

The Buffalo News (NY)

The Street Sweeper - AFB Media

TippNewsDaily (OH)

TMC.net

EPILOGUE

Thank you to Dan Poynter from Para.Pub.com who summarizes ideas about publicity and marketing so well, I have chosen to share his article "Writing Your Book is Just The Beginning."

Writing Your Book is Just the Beginning

by Dan Poynter

One of the greatest misconceptions harbored by writers is that the job is done when the book manuscript is mailed. While manuscript completion is a time to celebrate, it is also the time to switch hats. The book *writer* now becomes the book *promoter*.

A book is like an iceberg. The writing is the easier part; the 20% visible above the waterline. The promoting is the most important part and usually consumes even more time and money. The promoting is also often the part not anticipated by the author.

Bringing a book into the world is like bringing a child into the world—you are presented with an obligation to raise it. Now, fortunately, the obligation to your book is not a 20-year commitment and you do not have to send the book to college. But, you do have to let people know that you have books in your garage—or they will remain in your garage.

Any fool can write a book, it takes a genius to sell one. --Anon

As the author of the book, you have few choices. You are responsible for the promotion whether you self-publish or sell out to a publisher. If you abdicate your promotion responsibilities, your book will become an orphan. Yes, if the book is to be successful, the promotion is up to you.

Each book goes through four distinct stages. The author' responsibilities are to create the manuscript and promote the book. The publisher has the book manufactured and then distributes it to the Book Trade (wholesalers, bookstores and sometimes libraries).

Publishers do not promote books; they do little more than list your title in the catalogue. Ask any author who has been published by a publisher and he or she will probably complain "they didn't do anything!"

The Four Stages of a Book

Stage:	Writing	Producing	Distributing	Promoting
Responsibility:	Author	Publisher	Publisher	Author
Subcontract:		Printer	Distributor	

By now, you are wondering why you need the services of a publisher. You really don't. You can deal with one of the 24 digital-book printers or the 42 offset-book printers across North America. They will print and bind your book. These book printers specialize in manufacturing books.

They will provide price, service, and quality because they know what a book is supposed to look like. Any printer can produce a book, one way or another, but book printers specialize. They manufacture books only.

Finish the manuscript and then upload the ebook to Smashwords.com and Amazon/Kindle. That's it; you are "published." Next, set the type, layout the book and have 500 printed.

There isn't any reason why you can't shepherd your book through all four stages yourself.

By now you are probably wondering whether the well-known celebrity authors have to promote their own work. The ability to promote is one of the criteria a publisher assesses when considering a submission. Publishers want mediagenic authors.

For example, Frank McCourt, (*Angela's Ashes, Tis, Brotherhood,*) said he spent six months of each year on the road.

Most of the people being interviewed on radio and television are recently -published authors. And, why not? They are celebrities and are experts on their subjects. People find authors fascinating.

You should devote a minimum of one year to the distribution and promotion of your first book to make sure it gets its fair share of your time and energy. Too often, an author will write a book, have it printed, start on the distribution and then get distracted with the writing of another book. The first book then becomes an orphan and it does not get onto the hands of willing, potential buyers.

Every one of your books will provide a learning experience in each the four stages. The second time around will be easier and the third time easier still. So you may put just nine months between books two and three, six months between books three and four, and so on.

The secret to successful publishing is not to produce more books but to effectively market those books already published.

Writing the book is the easy part of the process. As the author (and the parent) of your book, you have an obligation to provide it with the best opportunity for growth. You must do more than just write the book. Look under the water.

Dan Poynter does not want you to die with a book still inside you. You have the ingredients and he has your recipe. Dan has written more than 130 books since 1969 including *Writing Nonfiction* and *The Self-Publishing Manual*. For more help on book writing, see http://ParaPub.com.

© 2014

www.ingramcontent.com/pod-product-compliance
Lightning Source LLC
Chambersburg PA
CBHW081310170526
45166CB00011B/3477